What people are saying about

The Norns, Weavers of Fate and Magick

The Norns, Weavers of Fate and Magick is a fascinating look at the Norse spirits of fate, which weaves together myth, history, and personal experience to create one nuanced understanding of these complex beings. The perfect book for anyone seeking to learn about the Norns or to go deeper in understanding them and their importance in our lives.
Morgan Daimler, author of *Pantheon: The Norse*

Irisanya Moon's work is an enjoyable exploration of the Norns. She combines academic source material with years of practical experience in an effective, engaging guide for working with the Wyrd Sisters.
Ryan Smith, author of *The Way of Fire and Ice: The Living Tradition of Norse Paganism*

The three Norns were a group of female supernatural beings who, within Nordic mythology, weave fate and control the fate of the cosmos, as well as the destinies of mortals and Gods alike. In *The Norns, Weavers of Fate and Magick*, Irisanya Moon introduces the reader to these beings, Urdr, Verdandi, and Skuld, each of whom have their own specific function and purpose that tend to weave in and out of our human lives. An invitation to explore and work with each Norn is offered to those who are interested in diving deeper into working with these beings.
Frances Billinghurst, author of *Encountering the Dark Goddess: A Journey into the Shadow Realms*, *Contemporary Witchcraft: Foundational Practices for a Magical Life* an*~~ ~~* *~~H~~*~~ Silver B~~
Guide to the Moon, Myth and Magic

The Norns, Weavers of Fate and Magick by Irisanya Moon leads a reader into working with the Norns through self-reflection, story, and ritual workings. An excellent guidebook into the magic of destiny that any ritualist will enjoy.

Jennifer Teixeira, author of *Pagan Portals - Temple of the Bones: Rituals to the Goddess Hekate*

Irisanya presents a thorough examination of the Norns, rooted in personal experience and research, yet open enough for readers to form their own relationship with them. In *The Norns, Weavers of Fate and Magick*, she does an excellent job of making the mythical personal, by teaching readers to work through personal wyrd for collective good.

S. Kelley Harrell, author of *Runic Book of Days*

Pagan Portals
The Norns

Weavers of Fate and Magick

Pagan Portals
The Norns

Weavers of Fate and Magick

Irisanya Moon

MOON
BOOKS
Winchester, UK
Washington, USA

JOHN HUNT PUBLISHING

First published by Moon Books, 2023
Moon Books is an imprint of John Hunt Publishing Ltd., No. 3 East Street, Alresford
Hampshire SO24 9EE, UK
office@jhpbooks.net
www.johnhuntpublishing.com
www.moon-books.net

For distributor details and how to order please visit the 'Ordering' section on our website.

Text copyright: Irisanya Moon 2022

ISBN: 978 1 78904 910 7
978 1 78904 911 4 (ebook)
Library of Congress Control Number: 2022939992

A CIP catalogue record for this book is available from the British Library.

Design: Matthew Greenfield

UK: Printed and bound by CPI Group (UK) Ltd, Croydon, CR0 4YY
Printed in North America by CPI GPS partners

We operate a distinctive and ethical publishing philosophy in all areas of our business, from our global network of authors to production and worldwide distribution.

Contents

We meet the Norns at the base of the World Tree, the one who weaves, the one who measures, and the one who cuts. With Urd, Verdandi, and Skuld, we travel across time and come to meet ourselves as part of fate. And in this meeting, we join the weavers of destiny and encounter the wyrd.

Acknowledgments

There are parts of my life that have found themselves to be a part of a greater tapestry, but only upon reflection and return to memory. People in my life have come and gone, like tides and shadows. Like seasons and promises.

I want to acknowledge those beings. The humans that have continued to support me closely and from afar, even when I was less than understandable. More than confusing and often absent.

While I wander away from the fate before me, I only wander a little while, a few steps from the place where I will surely arrive. I just need to be away at times. Perhaps that is the place of a writer and human living in these times that have also arrived – just as they were destined to do.

I'm still not sure I believe in destiny or fate or all the liminal space between these two ideas – betwixt and between. But what I know is that even in all my confusion and all of my wondering, I am more often glad to be in the place I am in.

I may not know or understand what will happen next, but the magick of the Norns reminds me that it all has a place. It may not have a meaning yet, nor a purpose or a direction, but it all has a place.

So, no matter where I am, I am home.

I thank the ones who have held my hand along the way.

I thank those who are waiting to take my hand.

Author's Note

One thing I like to say in all my books about deities is this: take what you will and leave the rest. I know that authors look like authorities at all times. We might look like we know everything, and each offering is another brick in a wall of history or myth. But we only know what we know by what we find, what we seek to find, and what we understand at that moment. More often than not, we offer what is resonant for us and what has touched us personally.

Tomorrow is often different. Thankfully. The next day might offer another piece of unburied history or reflection. More context. Less influence from whatever person benefitted from a story being told a certain way. All I can tell you is that this book is how I know the Norns. How I've known them since starting to work with them more than a decade ago. How I've worked with them up until this point of my life. Because, like any relationship, I imagine things will change. I will know more and grow more and expand my experience.

I know the godds[1] by how they show up for me, versus how they are written about – or what I hear from others. Like any relationship, this is how I get to know people. I experience godds the way they are for me. (And are the Norns even godds? That is up for debate too.)

As you will notice in this book, I go to sources to learn more about what others think about the Norns, but I don't want to rest my opinions in any one author's or academic's lap. What I read is interesting. What I learn is fascinating. And I do have moments where I read one thing – and experience it differently.

This is not a dismissal of anyone else's experience, far from it. Instead, I offer the idea that my experience, background, and current personal awareness all color and inform how I see anyone in my life. And the godds are no different. My life informs my perspective. With more life lived, more perspective. (Or maybe not.) And how can I ever offer a complete understanding of anything? Or a complete view? There are many more books to be written. Translations to compile. Transcendent experiences to have.

Also, the Norns are everywhere. They are the energies between moments and of moments. To me, they are the everything that touches everything. That is not easily contained in words. Or pages. Or research. But I will try.

Take a breath with me. And perhaps begin to feel the threads of time dance across your face and even your heart. Feel how you are already connected to the great mystery of what was, what is, and what is becoming. And maybe more.

Introduction

The tree stood in the center. A holiday tree from someone's yard or home. It's hard to remember today. So many years later. So many rituals and gatherings later. It leaned to one side as it was moved into the hall. And folks who gathered started to dance around it as the drums played. The night was rainy and dark, or at least my mind remembers it that way. Samhain, though not the exact date. The season filled with the death of promises and beings. The world still and unknown.

We walked around the space of a community hall, each holding words that wove a trance across time and space and onto the ancestors. I stepped between time at that moment. And in other encounters to come. I don't remember if we'd planned it or if it just happened, but what I do know is that three humans dropped away and filled their bodies up with the energy of fate.

Weave. Measure. Cut. Weave. Measure. Cut. Weave. Measure. Cut.

I remember weaving a piece of gray wool between my fingers, again and again, a black line of paint down the middle of my face, obscuring the shape of my lips. Hiding me and, at the same time, opening me to the possibility of something unknowable. My lips were black. My eyes met everyone who passed me, but they were not my eyes.

Truth be told, I'm not entirely clear when the Norns first came into my life. I have a vague sense, but no shocking vision comes to mind today. It was slow, subtle, and mainly influenced by a coven I used to be in.

There were three of us, after all. And in the number three, it was easy to contemplate the Muses, the Fates, facets of Brigid, and the Norns. It made sense to want to be a part of a group

1

of energies that held each other and who were able to have an impact on the lives of others. (Or maybe it was *Charmed*.) We called ourselves the Wyrd Sisters, though every time I wrote our next meeting date in a calendar, I always spelled it 'Systers.' Oh, how times have changed.

What I can recall clearly is how it felt like fate had brought us three together. We hadn't known each other before a weekend class on foundational magick, but we came together shortly after. Like a gentle relationship, a quiet recollection of a bond that, to me, seemed older and comfortable. Before long, we were weaving magick together in conversations and tears and dancing and laughter.

Our time together included long cloaks and spinning around the fire in the woods. The magick of that moment caused the fire to spark and crash at just the right moment. Or that Samhain when the three of us invoked the Norns and held the energy of the one that resonated most with us. We all had one that aligned with our magick at that time.

I say all of this not to have you indulge in my nostalgia, but rather to offer the way time weaves stories across lives, brings people together, and then sets them on another strand. Another timeline and another path. That coven is a faded memory. A smile arrives when I think back. But it is not woven in the same way. The threads are still there, but looser and wider and connected more closely to other places and people.

One of the things you must know at this point of your new journey with the Norns is that they promise nothing. But also, they offer everything. And they never say it will be simple or easy. In fact, they weave only possibility. What you do with that is up to you. Also, it might not be up to you.

For you are a part and a place and a dream and a desire. None of it will make sense. Sometimes you will scream at the unknowing and the hastening of time. But you will also take a step forward in the realization that you are heading in the exact right direction.

Chapter 1

Meeting the Norns

I know that an ash-tree stands called Yggdrasil,
a high tree, soaked with shining loam;
from there come the dews which fall in the valley,
ever green, it stands over the well of fate.

From there come three girls, knowing a great deal,
from the lake which stands under the tree;
Fated one is called, Becoming another–
they carved on wooden slips–Must-be the third;
they set down laws, they chose lives,
for the sons of men the fates of men.
The Poetic Edda, translated by Carolyne Larrington

The Norns

How do you define or explain those that hold time? That's a great question. A bold question. A question that is hard to answer when there are few mentions of the Norns in texts. However, as you will see, there are more mentions than are often shared.

Some say, 'collective female spirits'[2] or those who "speak repeatedly of the judgment or verdict of the norns, and this means death or a life lived out, so that death is imminent."[3] A common meaning for norn in modern Icelandic is 'witch' or 'hag'.[4]

Some books would tell you that the Norns are demi-godds. Some would tell you they were never godds. Some would tell you they live in a hall at the base of the World Tree. What you will need to know is that the Norns are often depicted as three beings, some say giantesses, some say deities, and some say shadowy figures. And some say they are just three of many.

I think this discussion is interesting, though potentially

3

unnecessary, to move forward in any relationship building with these beings. If the Norns are the ones tasked with the fates of man and the concept of wyrd also includes the godds, it seems to me that the Norns are everywhere and all the time.

Norn (plural, Nornir): a word that might be to twine or weave. It might also mean to secretly communicate. At the same time, there is disagreement about the weaving.

They are the past, the present, the future, and all that is in between. The Norns are the beginning and the ending, but also ever-present and beyond the memory of time and the flight of ravens. If we use Larrington's translation, for now, this is who the Norns are:

- Fated = Urd
- Becoming = Verdandi
- Must-be = Skuld

There are other interpretations of their names and their roles, which we will go into more detail throughout this book. In addition, there are many ways to spell and pronounce their names, depending on the language, translation, etc. They (Urd, Verdandi, Skuld) are also called Fate, Being, and Necessity.[5] The Norns are the ones who create the fates of humankind. They are tasked with the creation of each destiny, measuring its length, and cutting it from the web of life. They are also called the Wyrd Sisters due to their part in the creation of the wyrd, or fate and destiny.

Each Norn offers a piece of the movement of time. And without going into too much detail yet, I want to offer that while humans perceive time as being linear, with a start and an end, the Norns seem to provide the possibility that time is much more expansive – and malleable.

Some would say that the most crucial role of the Norns is not about the weaving of fate, but rather about watering the World

Tree so that it doesn't rot. In some translations and studies, the Norns will take water from the Well of Urd to water the tree, but they will also take moist clay and earth to further help the tree be healthy and green. And as Per Bek-Pedersen observes:

> Skaldic references to the nornir often associate them with transitional situations, typically with violent death or with battle, but different sources nonetheless emphasize different aspects of their nature.[6]

The Norns are also the ones who attend each birth with the thread of life that will be woven into the Web of Wyrd, to place each human into the stretch of time and destiny.

A Brief Bit of Norse Mythology for Context

We begin this journey (or continue) with the sight of the Norns at the base of the World Tree, Yggdrasil. It will help to start with a bit of background into Norse mythology, though we will only touch on it tangentially as there are many other books that cover those beings and lands in detail. Knowing a little about the vision of where the Norns are will help in understanding their presence.

Creation Story

To set the scene of the Norns, the world began without anything, as an abyss and chaos called Ginnungagap. It was quiet and dark and rested between Fire (Muspelheim) and Ice (Niflheim). The fires and the ice crept toward each other over time until they met in the gap, and the melted ice formed into Ymir, a giant and hermaphrodite, who birthed more and more giants from his armpits as he slept. At the same time, the frost melted, and a cow emerged (Audhumla) to nourish Ymir with her milk.

Audhumla licked the salt in the ice and uncovered the first

of the Aesir group of gods (Buri), who birthed beings that eventually birthed Odin and his brothers. Odin and his siblings killed Ymir and created the oceans, soil, vegetation, and sky. Eventually, the first man and woman were created from two tree trunks, and they built a wall around Midgard to protect them from the giants. Thus was the world of men created.

Yggdrasil

Yggdrasil is the ash tree that extends across many worlds (which are referenced in different ways by different scholars, with subsets for certain beings and times), but a concise way to explain for now is:

- Upper: Asgard – the realm of the godds
- Middle: Midgard – the realm of humankind
- Lower: Hel – the underworld

The tree connects the worlds and allows for movement across the lands. There are creatures and other beings that live in all the lands and all between. This is the place of godds, where they communicate and meet to make decisions. At Ragnarok, the last time of godds and men, the tree is shaken and damaged, but it lives on as a source of life for the new time.

Again, if you've been studying Norse mythology for a longer period, you will recognize how I have abbreviated this part. If you want to learn more, there are resources at the end of this book. The shorter version is not out of irreverence, but rather to offer more space to the Norns as they are.

In addition, I will not be clearing up 'how to pronounce that' in this book. There are multiple pronunciations of each name, depending on the source and the translation. I invite you to spend time researching what resonates with you and what seems to be consistent in your study.

Before You Go Further...

One of the most wondrous things about humans is our ability to find connections and overlap in the things we learn. We are meaning-makers who take pieces of experience and try to make them make sense. For example, you have probably already wondered (or not) about the Roman Fates (Moirai) or the Muses or the Roman Parcae or other similar groups of women-appearing beings or godds that have some hand in the fate of humans. After all, the Morai are labeled The Spinner (Klotho), The Apportioner (Lachesis), and The Inevitable (Atropos).[7] They do sound awfully similar.

I am not one to say that something isn't related at all or that it could never be. But I also do not want to conflate these beings. I do not want to say that because some beings appear to have similar tasks, they are the same. I also do not want to look at the mysteries of the Norns through the eyes of another culture – at least not in this book.

So, if you've been thinking, Hmm. These beings seem like _____. You're right. But I don't think they're the same. Just as one might say that since Venus and Aphrodite have a lot in common, they must be two versions of the same thing. However, I also want to offer the possibility that if you resonate with the Fates or other similar groups of beings, why not see what they have to offer you?

I'm personally a polytheist, so I work with many godds, many names, and many energies. I also believe that godds can stand on their own without comparison to another. At least in magickal practice. In addition, as a modern practitioner, I look at things through my modern, personal lens.

Trance: Stepping into the Worlds of the Norns

Before we go further, I invite the opportunity to sit with the Norns for a while by traveling to the World Tree to meet them. You can choose to read this piece into a voice recorder to play back to yourself or have someone read it to you. Or you can choose to read it once and take yourself on the journey in a way that feels right to you.

To begin, you will want to get comfortable and be in a place where you will not be interrupted. This might look like lying down or sitting in a comfortable seat. You want to remain alert and feel safe wherever you are. It's not wise to do a trance while driving, for example.

I invite you to close your eyes if that feels good.

Give yourself permission to relax and let go of the worries of the world for a short time. It can help to breathe a bit more deeply or to slowly scan your body for places of tension. Allow yourself to release any tight spots or places of awareness that have wandered off into the future or the past.

You might start by scanning your feet and legs for any tension. You can breathe into that and let what doesn't need to be there drop, sink, and fall away. Then you may move to the hips and the pelvic bowl, again scanning for any tension, worry, or expectation. Allowing anything that doesn't need to be there to drop, sink, and fall away. Moving to the space of your gut and stomach, all the way up your rib cage and around your courageous heart. Briefly scan for any points of tension or tightness. And allow anything that doesn't need to be there to drop, sink, and fall away. Traveling the space of your shoulders and down your arms from shoulder blade to elbow and fingertips. Again, noticing any tension and inviting it to drop, sink, and fall away.

Moving to the space of the threat and the space of the jawbone and face, along the curve of the eyes and along the forehead, all the way to the top of the head to the space that was soft when you were born, allowing anything that doesn't need to be here right now to drop, sink, and fall away. Give yourself permission to be present and grounded and calm and safe for the journey forward, knowing you hold yourself and that you are deeply loved by the universe.

Easily, you open your mind's eye, the awareness that is uniquely you, and you spread it out like a blanket or a cloth. It expands beyond what you know right now, and it unfurls to the place of the World Tree. You can see the great trunk and branches of this sacred tree. Take a moment to witness this magick and how it towers over and around. You might begin to see different beings and creatures. You might begin to feel other sensations and hear sounds.

And somehow, you know exactly where to turn your attention to find the base of the tree. You might begin to hear the water from the well. You might start to hear the weaving of the threads of fate. You might begin to see the Norns doing what they do, moment after moment, birth after birth, death after death.

You may choose to go right up to them. Or they might choose to call to you. Or something else. I invite you to think about their names: Urd, Verdandi, and Skuld. I invite you to travel to them and see what they might offer today. What do they have to say or share or show? What do they look like? What do they feel like? What happens in this first of many meetings?

Take as long as you like to be here with them, knowing that you can always return in the future. Once you feel your time has come to a close, you might want to thank the Norns for their presence and for their wisdom. You may want to offer them a gift or some other token of appreciation.

Come back to the place where you began, the way that you traveled. And arrive at the place where you opened up your attention and *awareness. Bring that back into yourself. Bring that back to the place of your head and body, wrapping it back into you and allowing each part of your body to wake up and become more aware of the room you are in.*

You can say the names of all of your body parts to bring them back into your conscious mind, from head to jaw to neck to fingers to elbows to shoulders and heart. From ribcage and gut and pelvic bowl to hips. From legs to ankles and then open your eyes if they've been closed.

Arrive back to yourself and take a few moments to collect any thoughts.

- Journal on what your experience was like, what it felt like, and what was surprising.
- You might choose to draw instead of writing if images make more sense to you.
- Or you could take a piece of yarn and hold that as you reflect on your experience.

Allow yourself to do what feels best and what feels right.

Chapter 2

Myths & Stories of the Norns

Three wise women
live there,
by that well
under that tree.
Urth is named one,
another is Verthandi,
the third is named Skuld.
They carve men's fates,
they determine destiny's laws,
they choose the lifespan
of every human child,
and how each life will end.
The Poetic Edda, translated and edited by Jackson Crawford

In my practice with godds from many pantheons, it is clear that not all beings have stories that place them in the action of the mythology. This is not necessarily a measure of their value in cosmology, but it does strike me as an interesting thing to consider. If there are no stories, how do we ground the godds in some sort of timeline? Do we need to? I'm not the one to answer that, as I think stories that are told and collected are forever influenced by those who are telling them. (As you have already seen and will see in the many translations of the *Poetic Edda*.)

In addition, I too am influencing the way that stories of the Norns are told since I have left out certain translations, and I have certainly not included all the possible thoughts on the Norns. I am offering my perspective based on the study I have done (up to this point) and my own personal experience/gnosis. Ask me again in a year what I think, and you might hear more nuance in my offerings. All of this is to say that the myths and stories of the Norns are sparse. They are usually only in a few lines of text. From there, we can expand the meaning of their presence based on the context, but since different translations offer different possibilities, we may not be correct.

As mentioned at the start of this book, I find the best approach is to take what makes sense for your personal practice – and leave the rest for another time or another human.

The First Poem of Helgi Hundingsbane

Night fell on the place, the norns came,
those who were to shape fate for the prince;
they said the prince should be famous
and that he'd be thought the best of warriors.

They twisted very strongly the strange of fate,
...in Bralund;
they prepared the golden thread
and fastened it in the middle of the moon's hall.

East and west they secured its ends,
the prince should have all the land between;
the kinswoman of Neri to the north
threw one fastening; she said she'd hold it for ever.
The Poetic Edda, translated by Carolyne Larrington

In the first part of the *Poetic Edda*, after the listing of the godds and the creation of the worlds, we come into the stories of significant people and battles. In this story, there is a war between groups because of not returning a dead body. At this point of the piece, the Norns seem to be brought in to talk about how this prince who had slain another is one they meant to be strong and famous in the history of man. The Norns seem to not only place this fate upon the prince but also to secure for him the lands as well as a kinswoman.

When I read this story, I think about how the Norns are often presented in a narrow space of overseeing fates, but rarely are they talked about as having any favor. In my early studies, the weaving of fate was more of a 'chance' thing or something that was not considered as having good or bad elements. But as we move into these small pieces where we see the Norns arrive and do what they do, it becomes clear that they are not just the holders of the wyrd, but they are also the ones who pronounce what the fate will be. Though 'good' and 'bad' is a bit too narrow and binary, it does seem clear to say that certain humans are set up for success, while others are not.

We can see how this plays out for those of us living in this time and our own lives. And we'll talk more about fate, wyrd, and oorlog in the next chapter.

The Lay of Regin

What is that fish which courses through the water,
which doesn't know how to avoid danger?
Your head you can save from hell;
Find the serpent's flame for me!

Andvari is my name, Oin is my father's name,
I have spent much time in the falls;
a norn of misfortune shaped my fate in the early days,
so that I have to spend my time in the water.
The Poetic Edda, translated by Carolyne Larrington, p.152

(Before moving on, a 'lay' in Old Norse is defined as a short lyric or poem that can be sung.)

Once again, the Norns are brought into a story with the

responsibility of creating the fate of a dwarf, Andvari. He speaks about how he was put into the water because the Norns put misfortune onto him. He lives under a waterfall and has the power to turn himself into a pike. One of the things to consider is how this story brings to light that the Norns had a hand in the fates of not only men, but also dwarves. This is one of the places where the translations have a hand in shaping the Norns as much as the text does. While they might be the ones who dole out men's fates, this may not be the entirety of their abilities or responsibilities.

The Lay of Fafnir

Fafnir said:

"The judgment of the norns you'll get in sight of land,
and the date of a fool;
you'll drown in the water even if you row in a breeze;
all fate is dangerous for the doomed man."

Sigurd said:

"Tell me, Fafnir, you are said to be wise
and to know a great deal;
which are those norns who go to those in need
and choose mothers over children in childbirth?"

Fafnir said:

"From very different tribes I think the norns came,
they are not of the same kin;
some are of the Aesir, some are of the elves,
some are daughters of Dvalin."
The Poetic Edda, translated by Carolyne Larrington, p.159

It was this snippet of the *Poetic Edda* that has presented a new view of the Norns in the space of time. Not only did Snorri Sturluson talk about the Norns being from different tribes, but this translation speaks to this possibility too. To me, this makes the idea of only three Norns a limited idea and likely a later addition/interpretation to the text. After all, this might be the influence of other later cultures that had the three-part groupings of supernatural figures.

Again, this section speaks to the idea of the Norns as those who are choosing the fates of men. While this is something we have already seen, the fates are also influenced by what has come before, so it sounds like the Norns do pass judgment in their roles. They are looking at what has already happened and then determining how that person's life will be.

The part that intrigues me more in this part is how the statement of the Norns choosing mothers over children is called out. The outrage of a mother living beyond her children is common, but not one that I thought would arrive in the text. But also, it talks about how the Norns go to those in need. Is there a way to call to the Norns? From what I have studied, there was no dedicated practice or worship of the Norns, but there does seem to be a possible way to ask for them to intercede.

A Short Poem about Sigurd

She had not known of any shame in her life,
nor of the injury that had befallen her,
no disgrace that was or could be imagined.
The terrible fates intervened in this.

Outside she sat alone, in the evening,
then quite openly she began to speak:
'I shall have Sigurd—or I shall die—
that young man I'll have in my arms

'The words I'm speaking now I'll be sorry for later,
Gudrun is his wife, and I am Gunnar's;
the hateful norns decreed this long torment for us.'
The Poetic Edda, translated by Carolyne Larrington, p.183

As someone who has long admired the Norns and worked with them as benevolent beings, the more I moved into the translations of the text, the more I began to see how the text tells a different tale. The Norns in this section are regarded as being 'terrible' and 'hateful' in their decisions and the impact of those decisions on the lives of men.

With this information in mind, I believe it wise to consider how this is an everyday experience for many people. The anger when something goes wrong (or several things go wrong) is something I understand. When life begins to present awful challenges and worries, I know I have shaken my hand at the sky and wondered whom I had angered. I'm not sure I honestly believe that for myself, but I do offer this: it is easier to blame the unseen than to accept the present moment. There are often so many decisions and actions that lead to each moment that it can seem as though something bigger is at play.

There are times when I want to blame something else, besides looking at my own participation in certain interactions and my place in their outcomes. Of course, this is not to say that there aren't bigger structures and powers in place that can impact our lives – oppression, patriarchy, capitalism, etc. But even that seems to be a part of the Norns' roles. If they are weaving fate based on actions and decisions that came before, the lasting power of these structures can seem as though it comes directly from their weaving.

At first, that seems like a losing battle, this weave that has been strung together for generations. However, I also offer that if threads have woven a tapestry that does not work, it also means the more threads of equity, justice, and interdependence we can weave now, the more we shift the fates of tomorrow.

The Lay of Atli

It would have been better, brother, if you'd come in a corslet,
with those helmets still groups round the hearth, to see the home
of Atli;
if you'd say in the saddle all through sun-bright days,
made the norns weep at the pale, doomed corpses,
taught Hun shield-maidens how to pull a plough,
and Atli himself you could have put in the snake-pit;
now that snake pit is ready for you.
The Poetic Edda, translated by Carolyne Larrington, p.213

I'm leaving a lot of context out of this story, to be sure. After all, Atli is often translated as Atilla the Hun. What you may also want to remember is that some of the *Poetic Edda* are fragments, so there might be context no one has access to anymore. This is a revenge story, as Atli is slain by his wife in retaliation for him killing her brothers.

I brought out this piece to show how the Norns were also written about as though they were human-like in their emotions. They were not just solid, staid beings who were not impacted by the human condition. In this case, the reality of death. Seeing the Norns as beings who were acknowledged as being a part of everyday life, those who might weep upon the corpses is also interesting when you remember the Norns would already know they were to die and the manner of their death. Yet, they still weep.

What the Stories Have to Offer

As you have already recognized, I talk about how the stories offer different insights into the Norns, but they are limited by the translations and the pieces of the *Poetic Edda* are still available. You have also noted that I only used one translation for these examples. This will limit the way the stories are heard, as much as they are told.

What I want to offer with this information, however, is the possibility that the more you can read about the Norns, the more you can understand their place in your life. You may not be a heathen or someone who ascribes to the Norse practice of magick, which is fine. But when getting to know any being or any deity who might become a working relationship, the more you can learn, the more you can deepen that relationship.

I have a list of resources in the back of this book, as well as websites that I've found helpful. But here are the places where I think people should begin if they want to learn more about any deities: original texts. For Norse mythology, this starts with the *Prose Edda* and the *Poetic Edda*. These texts, while missing some pieces, are the foundation for learning about the godds and the myths. In terms of the best translations, I think you need to make that decision for yourself. The more you read, the more you will learn which translations make the most sense for you. I don't like all translations as some are missing pieces, which I think are essential to the overall understanding of Norse mythology. I also say this because I've worked with heathens and seasoned practitioners of Norse magick.

The stories offer us context, always. Translations offer us possibilities for how things were. But as with any retelling of any story, the storyteller has an impact on what arrives on the pages. Stories are starting points and roadmaps, but we still need to take the journey for ourselves.

Practice: Entering the Stories

One of the magickal practices I use in my work with deities is to step into the stories whenever I can. This can look like reading the stories and seeing them in my mind to better understand each of the characters and how they interact. For those who like to use their mind to enter these places, that makes a lot of sense. For others, it might look like acting out the stories to understand how these movements and actions feel. I personally ascribe to a more embodied practice whenever possible. So, this is what I would invite as a practice.

Start by picking a story and reading it to yourself a few times until you understand the basic flow and movement. You don't need to memorize it, but it can help to understand it before you begin any movement. Sit or stand up, as your body allows. Read the story aloud to yourself and move your body in the way you imagine each character to move. You don't have to worry about getting it right, instead, focus on what feels accurate to you. This doesn't have to be a rushed practice and you can always start again if you feel you need to try a new movement. You can also tell the story as you understand it versus following a text word for word.

(When you do that, I encourage you to write down your version of the story for review later. You might notice your interpretation offers information about your personal relationship to what's happening in the story. For example, if you notice you side with a particular person in the story or add to their experience, this might be something to journal on more later as it might be a place of growth or challenge for your personal life.)

The point is to bring the story into your body to find out what the characters might have felt when certain things happened. As you do this, you will bring in an understanding that might inform the way things have been written. For example, when you read a story about how a person is upset about the cruelty of the Norns, you can begin to sense where that landed in the body of that being.

What I find is that I not only deepen into and beyond what the words are offering, but my body relays messages in the way I react or resist. If there are parts of the story that cause me to tense up, that is a place I might want to ask why. If there are parts of the story where I relax, that is a place I might want to ask why. All of this is learning and information for your presence in the wyrd. In the threads of fate and how you might interact more effectively. How you might begin to pull on those threads in a way that impacts future generations.

Chapter 3

Acknowledging the Norse View of Fate & Destiny

Wise women,
live there,
three women, from the well
under the tree.

One is named Urd,
another is Verdandi,
the third is named Skuld;
they carve men's fates
on ash tablets,
they determine destiny's laws,
they select life,
they choose how
children's lives will go.
Voluspa, The Poetic Edda, (Wíghearðr T. Andrsson)

Fate (noun): the will or principle or determining cause by which things in general are believed to come to be as they are or events to happen as they do; an inevitable and often adverse outcome, condition, or end; final outcome, Merriam-Webster Dictionary.

Destiny (noun): something to which a person or thing is destined; fortune; a predetermined course of events often held to be an irresistible power or agency, Merriam-Webster Dictionary.

If there is one thing you walk away from this book with, it's this: no one escapes fate, not even the godds in Norse mythology. However, this is not to say that everything is fixed in stone, though fates are set by the Norns. As you have already learned, the Norns play a part in how fate is set, based on how decisions, circumstances, and other actions play out in the lives of humans and godds.

In the academic discussion of fate and its placement in Norse mythology and practice, you will come upon a few terms: wyrd/fate, oorlog/orlog, and hamingja. There are nuances between these words and there are ways that they overlap so that it can be confusing at first. I am going to go over a few different viewpoints to enable you to better understand how this might impact your work with the Norns. Recognize too the power of thinking about these words for yourself and looking to more writings to see what people continue to say. Again, I offer resources at the back of this book.

When you hear about the idea of mysterious beings weaving the fates of man, it can sound a little stark. It might sound like we don't have any part to play in our lives as humans. It can sound as though everything is already mapped out, so our actions and interactions are already waiting for us. As with so many conversations about fate and destiny, it's not simple. We must remember that this all opens up in the context of Norse mythology and it could just be a story to explain what happens in the world. Or you could have been fated to read this book at this time. And the Norns had a hand in it.

Many scholars will note that Norse mythology relies on the idea that everything, even the gods, was subject to fate. However, other research offers that this concept of fate may also be a predominantly Christian creation.[8] Let's talk about it.

Wyrd

One of the most important concepts in Norse mythology is the concept of the wyrd. Wyrd is an Anglo-Saxon word, and in *An Anglo-Saxon Dictionary*[9], the first definition is 'what happens' and then 'fate, fortune, chance.'

According to *An [Old] Icelandic-English Dictionary* by Richard Cleasby and Guðbrandur Vigfússon, wyrd translates to 'a weird, fate', and the Old Norse cognate is urðr. Sometimes that looks like Urd, a name for one of the Norns. The well that the Norns sit at is the Well of Urd.

More definitions of wyrd are from the *Oxford English Dictionary*: "the principle, power, or agency by which events are predetermined," "that which is destined or fated to happen to a particular person," "what one will do or suffer," and "a happening, event, occurrence."

According to Cat Heath, the concept of fate was already across the Indo-European world in cultures from Asia Minor to Syria and northwestern Europe, by way of a triad of spinning goddesses. (Sound familiar?)

I think the concept of wyrd gets strange and complicated for folks who have grown up in Western civilization's shadow of privilege and are accustomed to stories where people break free of the chains of their past and single-handedly shift their fate. Pull yourself up by your bootstraps and all. If you just work harder, you will get further. If you just try harder or want it more, you can get what you want. The ever-awful story of rugged individualism that the United States is so fond of worshipping.

I know I had some troubles navigating the idea of wyrd because it sounded like being born into certain circumstances narrowed my paths or prevented some from ever showing up. Or it gave me opportunities that others did not have. But this conversation discounts that wyrd is not just about you or me. Everyone has a part of the wyrd, like a web, like a large woven tapestry. My wyrd intersects with yours, perhaps. Yours intersects and pulls on mine. And all of this is what creates fate and destiny. Stay with me for a minute. It's not about overcoming fate. It's not about winning or doing what you need to do at the cost of all others. It's about recognizing your part in the wyrd. It's about knowing that your actions will impact you AND they will affect others. We're all in this wyrd together.

You might never know how someone else's fate will impact yours. But it can – and it will. You may never know how your kind or harsh word affected someone else's wyrd. What matters is how you act in the world, how you are in integrity and in collaboration with other humans.

The way I've explained it to people is that if my fate is determined and the people that I will know and love are already waiting for me, I do have a choice about how I move in my life. I can choose to be open to what is happening, to see the lessons, and to take on the learnings. I can choose to meet my fate in a way that is honorable and respectful of the collective versus just being out for myself.

The Norse didn't have the privilege of being self-serving. What they did would impact someone else. What they didn't do would affect someone else. There is an image of a web of wyrd that shows this interaction a bit more easily than words can. You can see how the image has lines that intersect and impact each other. If these were threads, you would pull on one and feel it in another section. If you loosen the hold on a thread or line, the other side will feel it.

Everyone holds a part of the web and the weave. It is not as simple as the conversation sometimes becomes. It's nuanced. It's intersectional. If you are fated to hold one thread, you will hold it no matter where you go and what you choose to do. And that thread will impact others as much as it affects you.

The other thing I might add to the conversation of wyrd is that it stretches out from the moment you are in right now, but also back in time. You are the culmination of your choices and words and actions. And even though it can seem as though what's happening now has come out of nowhere, more often than not, your present circumstance is brought about by something you chose (or didn't choose) to do in the past. What you have done in the last two days will impact where you are on this day.

To me, this is where the conversation of the Norns is most interesting and helpful. When we can think about what was, what is, and what must be, we can remember that everything counts and has an impact. One might remember the Butterfly Effect, in which the movement of a butterfly's wings could cause a storm on the other side of the world. (But this is not really what the MIT professor Edward Lorenz[10] meant, though pop culture has taken it in this direction.)

What might your actions today offer to yourself or others tomorrow? What have your actions or lack of action already caused?

Hamingja

This was a new word to me, though one that was already in the discussion of fate and wyrd – just not named until I happened upon *The Way of Fire and Ice* by Ryan Smith. In his book, he speaks of Hamingja as luck, skills, means, conditions, and what circumstances make up our life based on our birth.

To me, this is the place of what is often unchangeable. It is what is, what we were given and what we are offered as a place from which to move ahead in our lives. That said, these things impact how we move in the world. These circumstances not only put us into a particular place, but they can also keep us in a particular place. For example, if you are born into a certain area, you may only be able to get a certain job in a certain industry, which might keep you in the place where you were born, or it might take you away from that place because that industry moves.

All of the circumstances of your life can impact the capacity of your life. Or they can impact the perceived capacity that you have. I may only think the world includes _____ because of where I have grown up. But if I move away and experience more, I realize that my capacity and opportunity are wider.

This construct is one I know well as I grew up in the Midwest and my worldview continues to be impacted by that upbringing.

Even though I have not lived there in almost 20 years, I recognize that some of my limiting beliefs are the result of where I was born. It takes active unlearning and challenging myself to move away from where I have been.

I do not want this to come across as a 'change your mind, change your life' sort of platitude, but rather an instructive moment of remembering that actions matter too. You may have ideas in your mind that are limiting you. So, whenever you have a thought that seems to be getting in your way, it can help to ask how it benefits you and how it might be limited. Even better, ask the Norns to show you where that thread came from and where it might lead.

Oorlog

The idea of oorlog/orlog is defined in some places as primal law. According to Ryan Smith:

[Orlog is] all the things in life that have already been determined by past deeds beyond our control, existing elements of society that come about through the accumulation of many actions over time, or the consequences of all the actions.[11]

To me, oorlog seems to be a soup of possibility but flavored by decisions and actions. The Norns then shape the oorlog as they see the deeds that have been done by all that have ever lived. But just as each person who has lived has changed the oorlog soup to this point, the next person can change it too, even if it's not a big change or an obvious change.

The idea of oorlog is one that some people don't understand or know as well as wyrd. It is part of the conversation and one that is discussed at great length by Kari Tauring.

I describe it by using a spindle. Each of us is born with a spindle of thread spun by parents, grandparents, great grandparents ad infinitum. This thread is our öorlog. We cannot un-spin it, but we can look into it, review it, learn about it, and have memories that surface to help explain why some of the spin is strong and some is thin, lumpy, or even broken and tied back in. We can also choose to spin our strand differently. In Old Norse, there is no future tense. As with spinning, we are constantly creating past precedence for ourselves and others with whom we are connected. The choices we make can either increase our luck and strengthen our wyrd or decrease it, not just for ourselves but for our descendants, community members, and humanity.[12]

But, you say, isn't this wyrd? Yes and no. Wyrd is the great web into which we are all woven. We can choose to interact in the way that we do, depending on where we are and how we decide to interact. Oorlog includes the things that we have, no matter what we choose to do next. We all come with our histories and the decisions of our ancestors. We all come with stories and traumas. We come with things that will influence us, for better or for worse.

We can take time to heal the oorlog. We can go back and heal intergenerational patterns and traumas. We can decide to do something different than what was given to us at birth. We can decide that we will move in a new direction. Taking all of this together, there are a few things one might be able to conclude:

- Wyrd is complicated as people are complicated.
- We are all born into circumstances that can influence our decisions and life path.
- We are able to make decisions that can impact our movement in the world.
- Everyone's actions affect everyone else's lives.

While I may have simplified this for clarity and understanding, none of this is simple. If pressed for my take on all of this, here is what I say right now: I may not be able to choose my fate, but I can choose how I meet it.

Reflection: Sitting with Wyrd & Oorlog

Something that can be helpful is to consider your own life to this point. Take some time to think about what has brought you to the place you are now. Maybe think about who has brought you to the place you are now.

An exercise that can be helpful is to write down a list of major events in your life, good and bad, and everything in between. You might think of these things as pivotal points and times when your life shifted course. It can help to write these all out in the order they occurred, on a timeline, if that's helpful for you to track things easily.

Once you have listed out the different things that have happened, you might want to go back and write down the things that happened that you had no control over, e.g., your birth, when you moved with your family, family events and issues, natural disasters, other significant events, etc.

At this point, you might need to move to a bigger piece of paper. With this information, begin to think about who was with you during these points. This can help with the next part. Step back and notice what you see in the well of your memories and life.

- What are common themes?
- Who are the people that keep showing up?
- What led to your big decisions or course corrections in life?
- Are there any patterns in your decision-making?
- How have you moved toward or away from things that happened?
- Are there things that you tried to avoid, but they ended up happening anyway?

You can even get creative and use yard or string to connect events that seem related or events that seem to have the same people involved. What kind of web have you woven in your life already? What places might be places where your decisions had an impact on others? Are there patterns you want to step away from? Are there decisions you want to make differently the next time?

Even if the concept of wyrd and oorlog is still a little confusing for you, it's not important. After all, you are already in both. You are living your life the way it needs to be lived based on what you are aware of – and what you have known up to this point. But you can cultivate awareness. You can widen your view. You can shift perspective. You can step into something different.

Practice: What Small Action Can I Take

I can get caught up in the tension between 'small actions can't possibly matter' and 'oh no, my actions matter.' This has led me to many moments of feeling stuck and frozen. If this is something that resonates with you, I offer this practice.

I begin by sitting with my heart to see what change I want to make in the world. This can be simple, small, and local. It does not have to be large and far-reaching. Remember, all actions have an impact on the wyrd. ALL actions. What is the thing you want to impact in the world? For today? For tomorrow? For your lifetime? I have certain political and environmental issues I am passionate about. When I feel ineffective and small, I think about those issues and find small things I can do. My list might look like:

- Researching local groups who are supporting these causes.
- Donating a small amount of money or resources to that cause.
- Talking about this issue with others.

- Sharing social media posts.
- Attending protests or actions.
- Doing magickal work for that issue.

As you will see, none of these included packing up or devoting my entire life to one issue, at the expense of the rest of my life. Small actions matter. They create momentum. They create confidence. They create a positive impact on the wyrd and the threads that connect the beings in the world. With each decision you make to do SOMETHING, you have an effect. You create future change.

What's hard for me sometimes is knowing that it's likely I may not see the impact of my actions for years, if at all. I don't know how one class I teach might impact the future of a person whom I never see again. I just don't know. And that's weird/ wyrd.

What I can offer is that you try to take one small action right now or in the next day. While you may never know how you did good (or not), you can do something. We can always do something.

Chapter 4

Urd – What Was/Is

Thence wise maidens three betake them—
under spreading boughs their bower stands—
[Urth one is hight, the other, Verthanthi,
Skuld the third; they scores did cut,]
they laws did make, they lives did choose;
for the children of men they marked their fates
The Poetic Edda, translated by Lee M. Hollander

Author note: I often use 'she' as the Norns are most often pictured as
and described as women in the texts. I'm not sure they are gendered at
all but wanted to make this note before moving forward. I will also use
'they' in singular references and group references to the Norns.

Who is Urd?

It makes sense to begin with **Urd, Urth,** or **Urðr**. This is the being
that sits below the World Tree with the other Norns, the one who
is most often connected with the idea of fate. She is the one who
is also connected with the idea of 'was' or the past. Urd is often
pictured as the one that weaves the strings of oorlog together to
create the piece of thread that is measured for each person when
they come into the world.

Urd is there to create what will become life, one that might
become wondrous. They might be seen as the beginning of
this fate and life nonsense, but they are often rendered as an
old being who is sitting there, decrepit, having been there the
longest if they are in the past.

I would argue that Urd is not the one who is the oldest, as they
are creating the potential for lives which is also akin to a starting
point and something that is happening in every moment. People

are coming into the world at every moment, just as others leave at every moment. How does one determine this to be young or old?

The presence of Urd is the one that reminds us that fate and oorlog and hamingja exist in some way, even if we do not understand or accept it completely. There is truth in the way that time and life present themselves. Even in going back over our lives, we can see patterns (or we create patterns) that may have led us to these points right now.

I choose to see Urd as the one who wants the best for us and the world. They are the one who is sitting there, reviewing the threads of time and the way they connect. Urd is the one who determines what goes into each thread and what does not.

To me, this is such a responsibility and a task for a being to do. And, if I stop to think of my own life, I do this too. I consider my past and how I want to move ahead with the things that have happened – or if I want to find ways to heal into something new.

The Potential for Nonlinear Time

One thing I need to put into place is the concept of nonlinear time. While the Norns are so often depicted in a line of past, present, and future, this is a bit too simplistic. It's poetic, to be sure, but that poetry offers a wide interpretation. For me, if I picture the Norns in my head, I see them all doing their work at the same time. This means that as someone is born, someone dies, and someone else is living their life as best they can.

The threads are flying all over the place, stretching and loosening as each moment changes and offers birth and death. As each choice is made and choice is avoided. While each life can seem as though the only thing they're doing is advancing toward death, the web of wyrd has so much more to offer. It is constantly changing and reworking itself – not only by the powers of the Norns but also by the decisions each person makes.

Time is more easily understood by humans when it is sequential. But just as you have learned about fate, there is much more than the time that influences life. There are the decisions of others, the circumstances of others, and the fates of others. All happening at the same time.

What I do today might seem to only have a future-facing effect, but really, it is also impacting generations to come who are yet to be born. And what I do today impacts me today, as well as tomorrow.

I invite the possibility that time is something that loops and piles upon itself and while the clocks and calendars might tell us that things are heading in one direction and that we're running out of time, this web of fate is much more complicated. This web is wide enough to hold more possibilities than we can see or imagine.

The Well of Urd

According to translations of the *Poetic Edda*, the Well of Urd is the place at the base of the World Tree, the place of the Norns, and a place where the Norse godds have meetings. The godds sit around the well to make decisions and investigate the lives of men.

The well is also the water source that helps nourish the roots of Yggdrasil. In some translations, the water is mixed with mud and placed on the roots to keep them healthy and supple.

It is good to remember that Urd is another word for Fate, so this is the well of Fate. This is the place where the world continues to be held in its existence. Where the world sits, where the weavers of fate sit, and where the godds sit. It is an important place that is only mentioned briefly, but impacts all.

The Well of Urd is one of three wells in the cosmos. There is also Hvergelmir Well, a well that is said to have existed long before the worlds were created in fire and ice, and the Mimisbrunnr Well, the well of wisdom. This well is one that one could go to obtain knowledge and wisdom, but only if they made a sacrifice. It is at this well that Odin gave his eye to gain the wisdom of the runes.

My offering is that the Well of Urd is a reminder of the pool of fate and the place from which you can draw to nourish that fate, no matter what it might be. It's not so much that it is 'special' because of Urd, the Norn, but rather that it offers a focal point for nourishing and communicating with the godds.

What Does Urd Offer?

If you intend to work with the Norns, there is no 'right' Norn to begin with, nor do you need to work with all of them at once. From here, this is your journey and your fate to explore. Since the Norns were not worshipped as other godds (or honored at all in places of worship), these offerings of how to work with each one come from my own personal experience. The Norns might guide you in other directions too. (And when this happens, I encourage you to follow their whispers and weaves.)

Where Do You Come From?

When working with Urd, this is an opportunity to explore the places you come from. By knowing what you are born into and what fates might have been woven into your thread, you can begin to understand who you are in the world right now. This might be as specific as the family you come from, but also a wider exploration of the beliefs you come from, the lands, the languages, the past as you can know it, etc.

Urd invites you to look back and beyond what you think you already know. This might require connecting with others you haven't talked to in a while or asking more direct questions of those you have in your life today. By knowing where you come from, you can begin to see where you might be traveling next in this lifetime.

What Makes Up Your Circumstances

Urd is the being that looks down at the way your thread has been connected to so many others, others who had wishes, dreams, and desires, just as you do. I appreciate this invitation for examination because it is a necessary part of dismantling oppressive structures. When we do not look at the circumstances of our own lives and the lives of others, we can look too narrowly at the world.

What you have been born into not only impacts the decisions you can make, but it also impacts the decisions that are available to you. For me, Urd offers insight into the conversation about intersectionality. Not everyone is born into the same experience, even if they are born into the same neighborhood – or even the same family.

The threads are much more complicated and require attention to examine. The threads are heavier for some and lighter for others. However, this is all relative given the current culture that includes patriarchy, capitalism, and oppression. Some are impacted heavily by these structures, while others are supported by them.

Dismantling the structures of oppression requires the commitment to uncovering and understanding that people do not all have the same opportunities. Many are born into places that limit and seek to continue to hold them back.

What Has Brought You to This Point?

The energy of Urd is also an energy that invites the conversation of reviewing the people and resources that have brought you to this point so far.

I don't want this section to read like an explanation or lesson of optimism. What I do want to offer is that Urd has woven resources and resilience into the thread too. I invite the possibility that we can also honor those parts. We can also identify what talents and skills we have that can add to the web of the whole.

While there are ways in which resources can be limited, it might be possible to expand those resources with community care and mutual aid practices. By recognizing what has helped us to this point, we can bring that outward to help those beyond our own circles and communities.

Healing & Nourishing Across Timelines

The Norns as a group have helped me lean into the idea that time is not linear, and things are not as fixed as they can seem. To me, this means there is a possibility of healing and nourishing ourselves across all timelines. Urd is sitting by a well that can make sure the World Tree stays alive, but it takes daily watering.

What if the waters of our own attention might soak the places of our lives that are dried out in anger or sadness? What if there are ways to offer healing to those of our past who did not have the resources to make certain choices? What if there are ways to send healing and love to the places of our history that contain oppression and colonization?

This is not to minimize, ignore, or 'fix' the past. What has happened in the history of humankind is awful and there are not enough words to contain those horrors. At the same time, I feel it's important to offer healing back along those threads of fate. To send energy that might soften and shift the threads moving forward into the future. Urd will then have new things to weave into the threads, impacting all the worlds and threads.

Ancestry & History

While I've already talked about where you come from, I want to expand upon the idea of history and ancestry as stories versus just facts. Yes, you have a bloodline from which you spring, one that might make you proud or one that you may try to hide. You may not know the truth about your ancestry or your history. You may not be able to know, for any variety of reasons.

Let's expand into the stories that you tell yourself about

where you come from, whether they are rooted in fact or not. Urd invites us to look at the stories too, to look at the way we talk about our ancestry. Does it arrive with shame? Does it arrive with pride? Do the stories get whispered across generations? Or are the stories something that continues to be shared and celebrated?

Urd can be a being to tell these stories to. They can hold the complexity of how stories are told, just as they hold the threads of all beings when they are born.

Trance to Urd

For this practice, I invite you to either record this trance below or read it through and follow it in the way that makes the most sense for you. It will be best to do this in a quiet place, where you will not be interrupted.

As with all trances, you do not have to close your eyes or sit still. I like to do trances standing up and walking around or swaying, as when I lay down, I can fall asleep. (There is nothing wrong with falling asleep either. A beloved mentor of mine who passed away used to say that even when you fall asleep, you're still doing the work.)

Get into a space that makes sense for you and for your body. The important part is that you feel safe and comfortable. The important part is that you can go inward without tension or worry. The important part is that you can soften and lean into the possibility of gaining more information.

I invite you to relax your body progressively, working your way up from your toes to your head. You can choose to tense and then relax each part of the body, or you might choose to breathe in to acknowledge each body part and then breathe out to release any tension.

Starting with your toes and your ankles, take a moment to see what's happening in these spaces today, without judging or fixing, just noticing. And allow anything that doesn't need to be there to drop, sink, and fall away.

(pause)

Moving along the spaces of your calves, knees, and thighs, all the way up to your hips and within your pelvic bowl, take a moment to see what's happening in these spaces today, without judging or fixing, just noticing. And allow anything that doesn't need to be there to drop, sink, and fall away.

(pause)

Traveling to the space of your abdomen and your solar plexus and will, maybe even moving up and along the ribcage and each rib, until you find your courageous heart, take a moment to see what's happening in these spaces today, without judging or fixing, just noticing. And allow anything that doesn't need to be there to drop, sink, and fall away.

(pause)

Moving again, easily and gently, to the places of your shoulders, down each arm and elbow to the wrists and fingertips, take a moment to see what's happening in these spaces today, without judging or fixing, just noticing. And allow anything that doesn't need to be there to drop, sink, and fall away.

(pause)

Once more, easily moving to the place of your throat and neck, along the jawbone and around the eyes and forehead, traveling to the space at the top of your head, the space that was soft when you were born, take a moment to see what's happening in these spaces today, without judging or fixing, just noticing. And allow anything that doesn't need to be there to drop, sink, and fall away.

(pause)

From this relaxed and safe space, I invite you to widen your inner eye of awareness and knowing. You might think of this as opening up a sheet and spreading it out or taking a ball of yarn and unfurling it around you.

However, you do this, the opening and the widening will help you find a path to travel on. You may not see it but experience it. You may also see it and feel the texture beneath your feet. You may just become aware that you are asked to travel in a certain direction and destination.

With each step, you find yourself getting closer and closer to the World Tree again, to the place of the Norns. You might experience them welcoming you over or they might be very focused on their tasks. But as you get closer, you can begin to see that Urd is more prominent and more present for you.

They look to you and you can sit with them for a while. You might have questions, or you might simply listen to hear what Urd might offer you. Feel free to stay here for a few minutes to see what might happen.

(pause for a few minutes)

Knowing you will remember all you need to remember, thank Urd for their attention and for their work in your life. Remember you can always return to ask more questions or to get insight into what you have heard.

Travel back the way you arrived at this place, whatever path you took. Once you return to the place where you opened up your awareness, begin to pull that back in and closer to your body. Become aware of your body in the space you are in, bringing attention back to the spaces of your body once more – from your head to your toes.

You can do this quickly and gently, becoming more and more aware of your surroundings as you do. Once you are back in the present moment, you can feel the edges of your body and say your name aloud to call yourself back to yourself.

This is a great time to write anything down that may want to remember.

Suggestions for Working with Urd

As with any relationship, you might find other ways to relate to each other over time, but here are some starting points for working with Urd.

Learn & Know Your Circumstances

It makes sense to try to find out where you come from and what circumstances have played a part in your life. A practice that can be grounding might be to write down the circumstances you understand at this point of your life and then take a piece of thread, yarn, or string for each. As you think about each of these and their impact on your life, you might wind them together and see how they change the overall thread you've created.

This can be something you put on the altar to Urd and add to it as you think of more facets. Your thread is just one of many in the world and it has an impact on others. You might even want to do this practice with a trusted friend or in a coven to share the threads of your life.

Sit at the Well

The Well of Urd is a place to be nourished and held. This water can also help to nourish your being by acting as a place to meet with the godds.

Create a well – This well can be a small bowl or an extravagant well, or anything in between. What is important is that this is a place you sit at from time to time. After all, the Well of Urd is a meeting place for the godds. You might sit here in silence to see what might arrive or you might gaze into the well to see if there are images that present themselves to you.

Draw from the well – The Well of Urd is also the place where water is taken to nourish Yggdrasil, so you might take water from the well you have created and pour it on yourself. You might also take a few drops of water and place them on the parts of you that need nourishment the most, e.g., your heart, your head, your feet, etc.

Journal through the Threads

When I think of Urd, I think of all the stories she holds in her hands. She can see all of them and she can feel the way they weave with each other. For myself, that can be harder to hold in my own life as time seems so quick and even slippery.

Journaling is where I can hold onto my threads a bit more easily. This can be Morning Pages, as created by Julia Cameron, or something less structured. Morning Pages is a practice of writing three pages of free writing first thing every day without stopping. This not only collects the threads of your mind, but it also allows you to make room for new things with less clutter in your awareness.

I have also journaled about my days without prompts or a page count. To get more Urd-specific, you can choose from these prompts:

- What circumstances influenced today?
- How did my history lead to today or a specific event?
- How did fate show up in my life today?

You can also journal in the morning about the threads that brought you to the morning and then write later about what you learned or what surprised you. The more you journal, I find, the more you can see how your life weaves itself in ways that become clearer when you pay attention.

Notice the Impact

A practice you might add to journaling is a recognition of impact, the impact of your life and the lives of others. This can be as simple as answering two questions in your mind or in a journal:

- How did my actions help today?
- How did my actions harm today?

I do not want to assign morality to these questions, however. What I want to encourage you to take away from this is the idea that everything we do has some impact, perceived or not. While we strive not to harm anything or anyone, we inadvertently will and do.

Does this mean we are bad people? Does this mean we have had a cranky Norn at our birth? This means we can only change how we interact in the world when we understand how we impact it. We will always harm, but we also heal.

Magick with Urd

With Urd as the one who reminds us of what has been and what cannot be changed, I turn to candle magick to support my relationship with her. This is a different kind of candle magick from other spells you may have done. And if this is the first candle spell you've happened upon, it is a great starting point for your magickal practice.

What you need:

A tall taper candle in a holder or a 7-day candle in a glass container

A bowl

Water

A safe place for this to be for a long period of time (e.g., a bathtub, enclosed shower, sink, and anywhere a child or pet cannot play with it). Whether you create sacred space or not is up to you, but it can help to visualize a circle around the work you are doing; one that slows time and allows it to be respected and revered without outside interruption or influence.

Place the bowl in the space you have reserved for this work. Place the candle in the middle of the bowl. Pour water around the candle so there is a pool that it sits in. Turn your mind to the life you have lived up until this moment, with its joy and heartbreak, delight and despair. Think about what you cannot change and what has been given to you.

Light the candle and begin to stare into the flame, allowing your gaze to soften until it is blurred and between the worlds. As you do this, focus on the way the candle begins to show the passage of time. Notice it fall away. Even if you were to do something else in this moment, the time would still pass.

Ask Urd to sit with you, at the well and the flame that hastens the speed of the candle's life. Allow her to hold you and show you what needs to be shown. Allow her to be your witness and your guide to the knowing that some things cannot be changed. She might offer you ways to hold this truth. She might honor your tiredness and your resistance if that arrives. She might simply sit with you and witness anything that comes up.

When you are finished, you can step away from the candle

and the well, but let it continue to burn (if this can be done safely) until the candle goes out on its own. If you are not able to do this, you can blow it out and relight it when it's safe again. As much as possible, return to the candle to see how it has changed. Remember too how much you have changed in the time you have had in life so far. Remember too how you have started in one place but arrived in another. Allow this working to be a reminder of what is and how the past is always coming, close to the edge of the present and inviting you into its creation.

Chapter 5

Verdandi – What Is/Becoming

Thence come the maidens | mighty in wisdom,
Three from the dwelling | down 'neath the tree;
Urth is one named, | Verthanthi the next, –
On the wood they scored, – | and Skuld the third.
Laws they made there, and life allotted
To the sons of men, and set their fates.
The Poetic Edda, translated by Henry Adams Bellows

I stepped into the center of the space, with Verdandi on my heart. I'd asked her to be a part of my magick that night and to step into my body to reveal what needed to be revealed. In this ritual, I was tasked with bringing people into their present choices and energy. How do you show up? What do you know about this moment?

The complication of Verdandi is that she is not only sharp but also fleeting. Because of her present moment energy, every moment with her is quickly the past. Every time with her is over in a breath, so the practice of being present is something that requires preparation.

But when I was aspecting[13] Verdandi, you cannot have a plan. I let my mind wander away to a safe place and all I could do was see what arrived. It was harsh and scary. She reminded people that all of us will die, and that each moment is precious and something we cannot prepare for. We can only meet it and remember it. She yelled and screamed and asked people to look in a mirror to witness their present moment. Verdandi called out for each person to know themselves and to trust their moments like points on a string, in a weave of a life. What does your present moment do to the present moment of another being?

What does the present moment offer to the past and the future?

How can you ever stand in the present moment when you are looking at the past or worried about the future? What does it mean to be untethered to the unchangeable reality and the unknown future? Is it tension? Is it wonder? Is it awe? Is it possible?

Who is Verdandi?

I don't want to say I have a favorite Norn, but I also do. It's Verdandi.

Verdandi / Verthandi / Verðandi: She is the Norn that measures out the stretch of a life, the series of moments. Some say she is becoming; some say she is happening; some say she is the present.

When I see Verdandi in my mind and heart, I see her as the one who holds the thread up and examines it. She can see it for the complexity and the things that lead to moments. She holds the measure of the ways in which we show up and the ways in which we do not.

Verdandi is not just the middle of a life; she is a reminder that all of life is moments that become the past as quickly as we realize they are happening. And the moments feed our future, often more quickly than we realize. With each decision and each step in a direction, we create a future, built on the possibilities and the chances we take in the past.

While Verdandi can sound contemplative and a being that can instigate an existential crisis, she is the one that also reminds us that the smallest of thoughts and actions add up. She is the one that seems clearly linked to the idea of making the next right decision, culminating in a life that we can be proud of. A life that can feed the web of wyrd and the fates of humans to come.

What Does Verdandi Offer?

If Urd is the opening of eyes, then Verdandi is a deep breath and Skuld is the movement and momentum toward whatever comes next. Verdandi is the place of acknowledging the opportunity in each moment. She moves quickly and is sometimes described as a young Norn since she is always becoming new or something different.

She is my favorite Norn because she brings things into sharp focus by being a moment you can't quite capture and a reminder that everything matters. Even the things that seem like they shouldn't be important. To make that clearer: we only have moments in this life. What you do with them does matter.

Presence

Verdandi is the essence of presence. How can you come more fully into this moment to make it count? How can you be aware that this moment is one that is just as important as the one you're worried about? This is not to say that moments are lost by how they are used or acknowledged. And this is certainly not to say that you will remember all moments or do something big and important all the time. We don't. You won't. I certainly don't.

But she can teach us that being present will allow us to step fully into the life we want to create and experience. This is not an easy task, especially if we have had lives that have required us to be physically, emotionally, or spiritually absent from a moment to survive. Verdandi invites us to return to this moment, the safe moment.

Gratitude

Another lesson that you can take from Verdandi is gratitude. Stepping into the present moment, to what is becoming in each moment does take a measure of gratitude. It asks that we come to the moment in some sense of thanks for all that came before and all that will come next.

If we cannot or do not experience some semblance of gratitude, we would not keep going. For me, this was the biggest lesson. When I started to look for things to be grateful for in my life, it enabled me to come back into the present moment. This encouraged me and allowed me to want to be present. For too long, I wanted to travel back to good times or hope for better times in the future. Verdandi said, "Yes, but also right now."

Opportunity

When I come into the moment and the knowledge of the power of this moment, I can recognize the opportunity. I can realize that this moment offers me the possibility of a new choice or a new viewpoint. While I may not be proud of all of my moments (or many of them), I can choose something else in the next moment. I can choose to say something, or I can choose to remain silent. I can choose to act from the heart, or I can choose to act from logic.

These choices are not necessarily good or bad, better or worse. They are choices. Each moment is a breath and an opportunity to move in a direction that is forged by me along the measure of my life. While circumstances may dictate resources and available opportunities, I have power too.

Personal Power

Though sobering, Verdandi's primary influence for me (and perhaps you too) is the recognition that I am part of my own creation. My decisions, my directions, and my stories are all mine. While they felt burdensome for most of my life, these are also things that are of me and thus can be changed by me. I have magick. I have creativity. I can recognize and value my own power. I have the ability (most days) to not give my power over to others. I can make decisions based on what is best for me, even if it makes others mad or sad.

She helps me remember that I do not need rescue. I need the presence and the reminder that the moments that got me here are proud moments too. While many have been based on survival and reaction, I am still here. I have learned from these moments too. I can choose something else, to shift something else. To show up more fully for me.

Values & Boundaries

Because moments are so fleeting, fast, and furious, Verdandi is also the teacher of determining what you value. These become guideposts and street signs to lead the way to a moment that aligns with who I am. Though the practice of picking values can take time, even knowing a few can help you meet a moment with clarity. What if someone says something or does something that does not align with your values or boundaries? You can walk away from them in a moment. You can speak up at that moment. You can choose to do nothing at that moment.

Verdandi asks that you know yourself, as you are and as you are becoming. Meet your precious self in all their forms and fashions. The beauty of becoming is that it is a constant and insistent process. It can be exhausting, to be sure. But it is also beautiful and bold and willing to be wrong. After all, there is always another moment to try again.

Trance to Verdandi

For this trance, you can either record the writing below or read it a few times and follow it in a way that makes sense for you. I do recommend a quiet place for these sorts of workings. But that doesn't mean you can't go out into nature and trance with the present moment in that way.

You're also welcome to bundle up in blankets or sit in the bath. Whatever works for you to have a space that will keep you safe and comfortable. I do invite you to have a pen or pencil and paper to write things down as you travel during this trance. This will be a little different and it might help to stay grounded with some writing. But you also don't have to do that.

For this trance, I want to invite you to keep your eyes open as much as possible. If you think you might get distracted, have a focus point. This can be a candle, a picture of a Norn or related image, or a mirror to gaze into your own eyes. The key is to make sure you can be present as much as possible during this practice. (And if you get distracted or it becomes too intense, feel free to stop and come back.)

As you settle into the space and place that makes the most sense to you, allow your eyes to travel as they like. Whether you have chosen to look around or you have chosen to look in one place, let that be the thing you do right now. Let it call you into the moment and back to the moment where there is nothing before and nothing coming next.

It might take a little time to settle like a ship or a wave. You might notice yourself coming and going from the present moment and let that be absolutely fine. In fact, it might just be the thing you need today. It might be just the thing.

If breathing into your body feels good and grounding, begin to do that. This might be starting with the breath you have right now, the length and texture of it. It doesn't have to be a precise length or even measured; it can just be as it is. But the more you call attention to it, the more you may notice it slows down and evens out.

If breathing is not the thing that makes you feel calm, forget that. Instead, focus on an item in your place right now that helps you feel good. This might or might not be the focal point you have chosen. It might be a pretty picture or the pillow on your bed. It might be the outside through a window. It might be the smell of the coffee or tea in your place.

Some find that touching something soft and smooth can be soothing too. If that feels like it will call you to this present moment, move toward that. (And if you're not sure, you can try these things and see how they work for you. You might feel better choosing one or

51

moving back and forth as you attend to your present self.)

Once you have come to a place that feels grounded, I invite you to look in one direction and notice what is happening there. What does your body feel like? What does your breath do? What does your mind do? There is no judgment in this practice. Only noticing this particular moment. Call yourself into that moment. Write things down if you want. Or not. Draw and doodle if you want. Or not.

When you feel complete, move to another corner of the room or another direction. What does your body feel like? What does your breath do? What does your mind do? What arrives in your observation when you come into focus? What arrives when you intentionally direct your gaze and awareness?

As you feel complete here, move once more to another section of your space. You can choose to do this as many times as you like. Some like to go to each of the corners. Some like the corners and the above and below. Some want to move to different kinds of places, e.g., windows and doors. Work stuff and playthings.

The intention of this trance is to come into the present moment so deliberately and fiercely that you are one with it. You notice. You are part of it as your body and mind respond. There might be vastly different experiences in each area. You might have one experience that repeats. All of that is welcome. When you feel you have observed all that you can and all that you want to, as you are always in choice, come back to your body. Maybe give yourself a hug or something similar to help you feel back into your body. You really don't have to call yourself back to be present, as the goal was to stay here.

If you have been writing as the journey went along, take a moment to go back to your notes to see what you captured. How did those moments of deep presence feel? Did you want more? Did your brain want to stay in the present or did it want to wander away? What about your body? While you can always journey to Verdandi, she is always present, so she is always right there. In the moments. In the seconds and breaths and observations we usually pass right by.

Suggestions for Working with Verdandi

To work with the magick of Verdandi, we 'just' need to live in our moments. I need to be willing and practiced at dragging my brain back into the moment I have. The world is not set up for the present moment. It asks us to regret the past and worry about the future. Verdandi asks us to remember that both will take care of themselves, no matter what you do. Time will pass no matter what. What you do with each moment adds up to the way you impact the wyrd and the way you embrace your life.

Meditation

There are many, many ways to meditate and there are many meditation teachers who might offer you something that works better than what I offer. I invite you to find something that resonates with you. What is important, I think, is that you spend some time learning how to be at peace with the thoughts you will have. Meditation is not a practice of dismissing or removing thoughts, but rather about recognizing when they arrive and deciding not to attach to them.

Here's what works for me. I start by finding a place that is quiet and still. For me, that is often the moment after I wake up. I take a breath and I notice where my thoughts are. I don't place any judgment on them. I don't try to make them something else. I just notice them.

- Oh, that's stress.
- Oh, I seem to have some worry.

- Ah, anger is showing up early today.

By naming the thoughts, they become experiences. They become things that are a part of my awareness, but they do not need to offer harm or peace. They just arrive. An image that I've heard from several teachers is the image of leaves floating down a river. Maybe you can notice the leaves of your emotions and thoughts as things that float down the river, away from you.

If you notice a lot of thoughts, this makes sense. They likely have wanted your undivided attention. Give them attention, thank them for making themselves known, and then breathe them out or watch them float away. What you'll find is that the more you do this, the fewer thoughts arrive and the more you find stillness. It can be a little jarring, even worrisome, for some. (It was for me. I thought something was 'wrong' because I was calm.) Even that can be a moment of observation. Oh, here comes worry. Thanks worry for showing up and making yourself known.

You can meditate for as long as you like, noticing your thoughts, allowing them to come, and then allowing them to pass by. The more you practice, the more easily you will be able to stay present in the moment, rather than letting your thoughts take over.

Grounding

If meditation is not a practice that appeals to you (I know it took me a while), grounding can be another practice that helps bring you present. This can be as simple as stopping your body, holding a hand to your heart, and letting things become still. Maybe you picture a root dropping from the base of your spine or feet into the ground. The roots swirl around and deepen into the solidness of rock. The roots release anything that might feel or sound like worry. When the roots are deep enough, you might take a breath or pause. Settle.

From there, these roots can also travel up into your body and rest in your center, possibly below your belly button. Then the roots or your awareness can stretch up your body into your arms where the arms become branches that reach up into the sky. The branches can travel as high as you like until you feel the tension of being pulled down and pulled up. I was taught at this point to bring those branches or awareness down into my center again to feel the swirling of earth and sky. Grounded between.

Moment Reminders

If you have a smartphone or some other alarm system in your home, you can also expand your practice across your day. I have set up alarms to remind myself this: Am I in the moment right now? I set up several of these during my day. At those moments, I stop and answer the question honestly. Now, if you are concerned you might answer 'no' every time, you're not alone. More often than now, I am not present. But the more times I ask myself, the more I tend to be able to bring myself back quickly.

Practice, practice, practice.

Staying with Emotions

"When a person has a reaction to something in their environment, there's a 90-second chemical process that happens in the body; after that, any remaining emotional response is just the person choosing to stay in that emotional loop," so says Dr. Jill Bolte Taylor.[14]

What does this have to do with Verdandi? To be in this moment, it's helpful not to get swept up and carried away by stories. I invite you to consider what happens the next time you have a strong emotion, even if you don't know where it comes from. I invite you to take a moment to name whatever emotion is happening.

I feel anger. This is anger. I am feeling anger.

And instead of going into why you're angry, why you should

or should not get mad, why anger is shameful, etc., stop. Just repeat what you are feeling. What it is and nothing beyond that for 90 seconds. Then notice how you feel at the end of that time. When I do this, I realize I am still in the present moment and I can figure out what to do next, if anything. Sometimes, I'm just angry and that needs to move through me. Sometimes I'm sad and that needs to move through me.

This is not a perfect practice, of course. And I do get carried away. You will too. But perhaps when you remember Verdandi, you might try to arrive where she is: measuring the cords for the length of one's life. Not because of a reaction or a story, but because that's the task at hand.

Measurements of Your Life
Speaking of the measurements, another way to practice with Verdandi can be to take a measure of yard or cord or thread and sit with it. Look at how long it is and how it feels in your hands. What does it feel like when you pull it or let it relax between your fingers?

Take one end of the cord and think about your birth. Think about where you began and what you were born into. Perhaps thinking less of the story around it and more of the facts of your entrance into the world. Travel along the cord with other stories of your life, moving slowly as you're not at the other end just yet. What stories make up the measure of your life? What stories are happening right now? What moments have brought you to the place you are? What gifts and challenges inform this moment?

Magick with Verdandi
What you will need:

Mirror
Candle of any size
Grounded mind

Ideally, you will want to do this practice in a darkened room, but if that is not available, you can simply choose a place where you will not be interrupted and not use the candle. (As with anything I offer, do what works best for you and what calls to you.)

Light the candle and close your eyes. Sink into the self that knows who you are right now. Drop into the place of understanding how you are arriving at this moment. You might call to attention how your body feels without needing to change it or fix it. You might notice your breath, without trying to change it or fix it. Just arrive as you are and as you will. When you feel grounded and settled, you can choose to light a candle (or not) and hold a mirror to your face. You might also choose to simply look into a mirror on the wall. That's great too.

Open your eyes wide and investigate your face. Ask Verdandi to be with you in these moments. You might imagine her holding your shoulders or standing to your side. When you feel her presence, start to examine your face. Look around your face to see what is present right now. You can look at the texture, the color, and the way it moves when you arrange your face in different ways.

If you are lucky enough to have lived a length of time where you have lines and wrinkles to consider, look at those too. Think about how they settle into places of movement and expression. Think about how they arrive in places of weariness and tension. And look at the way you can meet your own gaze – or not.

Whether this is simple or if you have other feelings that arrive, ask Verdandi to be with you in the moments you share with her. These moments don't have to be dramatic. You don't even have to arrive at some more critical lesson or insight. All you need to do with this magick is to show up. Meet the moments. Enjoy being here and getting to know yourself.

You can choose to continue for as long as you like, even moving to different parts of your body to see what you experience. The goal is not to tell stories of your body or face.

The goal is to be present and perhaps to hold gratitude for these precious moments. If you can't conjure gratitude, then I invite the possibility of pretending to do so. In time, you may find gratitude is nearby when we pay close attention.

Chapter 6

Skuld – What Shall Be/Is Becoming

Thence come maidens, much knowing, three from the hall, which under that tree stands; Urd hight the one, the second Verdandi,—on a tablet they graved—Skuld the third. Laws they established, life allotted to the sons of men; destinies pronounced.
The Poetic Edda & The Prose Edda (Complete Edition) by Saemund Sigfusson (Author), Snorri Sturluson (Author), Benjamin Thorpe (Translator), I.A. Blackwell (Translator)

Whenever I have seen pictures of the Norns, they tend to be old, decrepit beings. And Skuld seems to be the one that is assigned the most years. But she is not just death, though she includes it. She also includes the result of fate. She also includes what happens because of everything that happens before. She is always right ahead of us, the next breath, the next heartbeat. Skuld is not just an ending; she is the culmination and the promise we give to ourselves by the manner of our choices and our luck.

Who is Skuld?

Skuld: the future, should, debt, becoming, what shall be.

Some translations of the Voluspa poem in the *Poetic Edda* name Skuld as not only one of the Norns, but also a Valkyrie. "Snorri attempts to rationalize this by describing Skuld as the youngest Norn, who rise to battle alongside the Valkyries, to help choose the slain."[15] Because Skuld is the one pictured cutting the threads and thus ending lives, it does make sense that she might be on the battlefield with those who have died in wars. In these passages, Skuld is also called the youngest of the Norns.

When we come back to the idea of fate and the idea that death might be predetermined, Skuld can often be seen as ominous and frightening. She is the one that is at the end. But sometimes people forget that she is also the one of everything after the present moment. That can be a long stretch of time too. Skuld enters the timeline of life as the culmination of decisions and actions (and inactions). She is the one who is becoming and arriving because of the things you did or did not do in your life.

To me, this brings up the essence of responsibility. While much is out of our control in life, there are things that have been influenced by what we choose in each moment. Whether we choose to talk to that person or ignore that person, we have made a choice that could have effects.

What happens in the future might also be the debt we pay for the things we did. The easiest example is the way we take care of our bodies and health. What we do now is what we will enjoy (or not) later. This is not to say that genetics aren't part of the equation or bad luck or other things I don't know because I am not a scientist, but this is to say that our choices have an impact. And we might be paying back for the things we didn't do when our future arrives.

Perhaps it is also wise to remember that what we have done in the past should lead to certain things...and sometimes it does not. You are not the only one who influences your future. There are many who are a part of the web of wyrd. And you can make the best choices for yourself, based on what you think might happen later. Or based on what you want to avoid later.

Skuld, to me, is the being that reminds me that I can prepare all I want, and things will still happen that I did not expect. Such is the measure of a life. But she is also the one that reminds me I have choices and that I have so many choices to make the best ones for me – and for the collective community.

What Does Skuld Offer?

To work with Skuld is to engage the mystery. It is to offer oneself to possibility and the idea that many threads make up a life. While you can do all you can, other factors may be at play. Other movements that push us in directions of our longing and away from our downfall, sometimes.

Possibility

One of the greatest gifts of Skuld is perspective. Because each moment feeds the future, there is always a new future ready to be born. There is always the possibility of something better on the other side of where you are. There is always the possibility of something more than you can imagine because it is not a reality yet. Humans are built with a bias for the negative[16]. We are built for survival and that means preparing for the absolute worst. But we are probably not being chased by tigers all the time. (Well, not literally.) We can open to something positive too.

There is great freedom in the wide-open of a life, even if it can also be overwhelming to consider. Just as great things can come, not-so-great things can also arrive. I know for myself; it has been a long stretch of terrible things in the last few years. However, my work with the Norns has allowed me to hold joy and wonder alongside these less-than-ideal moments.

An Examination of Regret

Because Skuld is associated with the ending of life, this is a great moment to think about regret. I know for myself that I spent much of my life saying that I regret nothing, that I don't worry about the past mistakes I've made. I was a different person and I know better now. And while that is true in most cases, it is also limiting.

Regret means we realize we made a mistake and admit it so we can learn from it. So we can do better in the future. Regret is healthy. I imagine Skuld stops us occasionally and reminds us to look at why we got to the place we are. And if the measure of our life is still stretched out, we can learn and move forward differently.

However, this requires examination and the willingness to set a life's choices before ourselves, to see them objectively and kindly. This requires us to name what has happened, perhaps forgive ourselves and others (though certainly not everyone) and expand into something new.

Gifts of Becoming

I genuinely believe that becoming is the scariest and most dizzying part of the Norns. When I am becoming, it makes everything matter. This moment. This decision and my indecision. If I hesitate, I am also deciding. If I say yes, I say no to something else. When I say no, I can say yes to something else. While we do not get all that we could get out of these short, precious lives, we might just be able to be more discerning in what we do to become all (or most of) what we hope to be.

From the time you began this page or this book, you were becoming someone. Perhaps nothing feels any different, but even as you are right now, you are moving ahead in your life. Your cells are changing. Your blood is moving from one place to another. You are digesting food into energy, coffee, or tea into energy. Water is leaving your body with every breath. You are an active organism of change and becoming. Even the smallest of changes are impacting whatever comes next.

Life's Preciousness

When we're talking about a goddess that holds death, we can realize the impermanence of this life business. We are the ones that not only get to live a life, but this life and its precious wonder will also be filled with death and grief and loss. The more we connect, the more we will lose. The less we connect, the more we lose.

This life is a full range of experiences, one that weaves something we might never expect. Make time to enjoy the places that make your heart sing. Honor the places that leave you broken. Honor the price you have paid and the debt you will continue to pay because of what you have done.

Trance into Becoming

Allowing your body to do what it needs to do to be comfortable and safe, find a way to be still and centered. By now, you will likely have a practice that works for you or enough trust that you can bring yourself back to wherever you need to be if you start to get ungrounded.

Arrive in the stillness and travel to the World Tree. Travel to the place of the sisters three. To the place where they continue to weave and spin, water and cut. Look around to see what is here now. What do you hear? What do you see? What do you sense? Has the place changed from before? Is it familiar? What do you know of time and life at this moment?

Widen your awareness or your eyes to focus on Skuld. This being of unknown nexts and endings. This godd of sacred measures lived and final cuts from the web. What might she have to offer you? What might she show or tell you? What might she inspire you to do or be next? What might Skuld teach you about endings? What might she offer you about the time before endings? What might she whisper about becoming? And about what you are becoming now?

You might choose to journal when you feel complete in this process. And you might also want to be still and quiet to consider what your body understands from this interaction too. While it might seem strange to offer this, try not to understand everything. Just collect phrases and images and textures of your experience. Let them be as they are, without interpretation. Let

63

them be still as they lay across the thread of your life right now.

Suggestions for Working with Skuld

The beauty of working with Skuld is that she has so many lessons. She might beckon you to unfold into gratitude about your life in the moment. She might remind you that each moment is creating the future, so it's time to evaluate your direction and longing. Or she might push you toward remembering that you only have one life, one that is measured to reach a certain year.

To paraphrase Mary Oliver: What will you do with this one wild and precious life?

Funeral for Losses

The magick you work with Skuld is personal. For me, it has often looked like a rite of passage, a working from here to there. I think of initiation, but I also think of death – which go hand in hand. What you were is not who you are, even if it sounds the same and looks the same. To move ahead, you will lose things and people and ideas. You will lose opportunities and connections.

I encourage you to have a ritual or a funeral for all that you have lost. You can do this by emulating funerals you have planned or attended before, or you can do something more straightforward. I like the idea of writing a eulogy for the thing(s) I have lost. I will talk about who they are, what they gave to me, what I didn't like (I'm a fan of honest eulogies), and how I will remember them.

For example:

Today, I want to celebrate the life of my friendship with Jane Smith. There were so many beautiful times until its end. I remember hiking to the redwoods, dancing under the stars, and having way too many cups of coffee. I celebrate the times around the fire when I burned my necklace, and we sang songs until we laughed. And I applaud the distance that grew, showing me how I had changed and needed different things. I learned that I needed to speak up for my needs and to reciprocate the kindness given. I will always remember you and honor you, but I also lay your memory down for the earth to compost and claim.

You might do a burial of the eulogy or burn it if it's written out. You can also just speak from the heart and mind. I think it's more powerful when you say things aloud and even more potent if you have a witness. And you can do this as often as you like, as much as feels good and necessary to lay the past to rest.

What Price Have You Paid?

When I first learned about the debt one pays in becoming the person they become, this made so many things click into place. While I used to scoff at the idea that 'nothing in life comes for free,' there is a truth to that. For this practice, you will want to have beads, pennies, stones, or some other assortment of small items. They don't have to be the same, but you do want to have a fair number of them. Also, a jar or a bowl will help, though any clear surface will work too.

Thinking over your life, consider what price you have paid to get to where you are right now. What have you sacrificed? What have you lost? Each time you think of something or someone, move one of the items to a pile or to the container. Continue this practice until you can't think of anything else. (And know you can return to this practice whenever you think of more.)

Look at the bowl or the pile of items. Look at all that you have paid. All the debt. All the things you may not remember in the everyday moments. Honor that sacrifice. That making holy to make way for the life that is still unfolding.

Writing an Obituary

Unsurprisingly, I think Skuld is the perfect Norn to help you write your obituary. This piece of writing might announce your death and be shared with others. Like a eulogy, it often talks about the person and their achievements. It might also include mentions of partners or family members.

For this practice, I invite you to write the obituary as though you died today versus in the future. Write about yourself and all that you have accomplished and want to share up to this point in your life. This writing doesn't have to be lengthy or too detailed, just long enough to showcase who you are and what you have brought into the world up until now.

When you're done, read it to yourself. Think about how you feel about your life until this moment. Does it feel complete? What else do you want to do? How can you plan to do the things you wish you could have put into the obituary? Contemplating death is a practice that can allow us to be fully alive. When we are realistic about the fact that life ends, we can pivot to fill our life with more things that bring us joy and purpose.

Witness Your Regrets

For this practice, you will need a piece of paper and a writing instrument. It can also help to have a timer or some way of watching the time. Take 10 minutes to write down every single regret that you can think of. This can be a list of things. Or it can be an explanation of things. It can be compiled in any way that makes sense to you. You might list things according to year or age or incident. You might write 'I regret' at the top of the page and list things as they come into your mind, big and small.

But take the whole time to do nothing but this exercise. Ideally, you would keep writing the whole time, however, you can also take breaks to breathe and stretch. Try not to pick up your phone or start another task. Just focus on the regrets, realizing you might not remember every single one.

Once you are done, close your eyes. Notice how you feel. Notice what this has brought up. Place a hand on any area of your body that needs attention or that feels grounding. And breathe. It can help to name the feeling you are having or that you think you are having.

I am sad. I am angry. I am overwhelmed.

Just repeat that to yourself. I am [insert the emotion]. Breathe and offer yourself kindness. Offer yourself presence. Attend to the feelings that arrive, without attaching a story or meaning. Once the feelings simmer down or settle, thank yourself for doing the best you could. Thank yourself for trying. Thank yourself for learning. Forgive yourself if that feels right and needed. Be kind to yourself.

Magick with Skuld

For this magickal experience, you will need a few things:

A divination tool (tarot deck, runes, oracle cards, etc.)
Your journal and something to write with

As I think of Skuld as the one who waits for our arrival in each moment as they always knew we were coming, they are a perfect being for divining into the future and its possibilities.

First, I encourage you to ask Skuld to sit with you and honor this practice. You might sit at a table and leave a chair open. Or you might have a picture or placeholder for Skuld beside you. Stop to think about a question you have for your future. Or about the future you have in mind. Or the next thing you want or need to happen in your life. Be bold with your question and specific. There is no need for vagueness.

When you have the question in your mind, take the divination tool and pull as many cards as you like to help you get an answer. I tend to pull three – one for the past, one for now, and one for the future. Or you could choose just one and then one more if you're not sure what the first one meant.

Since this is not a book on divination, what happens next in your interpretation is up to you. I invite you to look at the images you pull first before you look at the book that describes the meanings. See what the pictures have to say and show you. Ask Skuld what you should be seeing or noticing. Write down your impressions until you feel complete. And then close the place where you recorded them. Return to the notes in a day or two.

What is coming is always on its way, to be sure. And asking questions is not a practice of distrust or fear necessarily. It can be a practice of preparation. It can be a practice of opening to the knowledge that is all around us if only we'd just ask the right questions.

Chapter 7

Cultivating a Relationship with the Wyrd Sisters

When you see images and sculptures of the Norns, they come in a set of three. You are unlikely to see a piece that highlights only one Norn at a time. As a result, it might seem that this is how they should be met in your magickal practice. If you're looking for guidance here, I will offer this: work with the Norns as a group at once to see how they settle in your life and your practice. Find out how they interact and how they influence your life as you begin to understand each other better. From there, you might decide you have one 'favorite' Norn, as I have already admitted.

It might be that you want to work with one Norn for a while and then move on to working with another in another period of your life. It might very well be that I work with Verdandi for a certain period of my life before moving toward Skuld in the later part of my journey. Or not. It's all a personal decision and something only you can direct, a decision only you can make.

Starting Any Relationship

If you're interested in starting to work with the Norns, you're already well on your way. Whether you've been called to these beings or you've been tasked with working with them, you have already started the process of getting to know them.

While I've often been a person who doesn't really think hard about what the expectations of a relationship are at the start, I think this is shifting for me. When working with any gods, I think it's wise to start with a set of expectations and intentions. This doesn't have to be anything set in stone. You can always change your mind later. I like to call this practice putting your intentions 'in pencil' where they can be erased and adjusted, unlike other writing tools. Here are some questions to consider when starting:

- Why do you want to work with the Norns?
- What calls you to this work?
- What experiences have you had?
- What do you expect from this relationship?
- What are you willing to do in this relationship?
- Do you want things to be short-term or long-term?

The more you can define what you're looking for and why the more it will enrich your practice. If you can get clear, you can more easily adjust your actions and/or stop your practice if it's not working out the way you want. So often in magickal circles, and probably more often for those new to deity work, there seems to be a sense that there is a 'right' and 'wrong' way to do things. Or there is a sense that you will offend a godd if you decide to stop working with them.

For me, this is not possible or probable. Since I don't put godds on a pedestal (and I encourage you to consider this too), I believe there are many ways to build a relationship. And there will be mistakes along the way, just as there are many ways to build a relationship. You are a unique being who will see things in ways I cannot. You will know things in ways that I do not. In doing so, you will arrive at a relationship with the Norns in the way that you do. Thus, there is no right or wrong way to do it.

I also cannot believe that beings of time and destiny are the slightest bit worried or concerned about someone who stops working with them for any reason. Isn't it better to step back when you can't give what you need to give? Or step back when you realize you aren't as compatible as you thought you were? (If you've done any dating or tried to make friends, you can see how this all pertains to any and all relationships.)

I go into detail about this because pursuing a relationship

with the Norns is a bigger thing than collecting facts about them. And that's fine too. Start out this work together when you are ready. And when you can answer the 'why' of your pursuit in this particular direction. The more you can understand where you begin, the easier the journey will be as you move forward.

Building upon Your History

Like any good relationship, building a relationship takes time. It will take ongoing dedication to get to know them and to understand the Norns. Remember when you are working with those who weave fate and that stretch beyond the human understanding of past, present, and future, you are working with beings who have all the time in the world. They cannot be rushed.

What I offer is slow and steady relationship building that looks like daily contemplation. This might be reading the lines from the *Poetic Edda* about their arrival in the stories of the godds. You might choose to find different translations of their description to see what that offers and if there is one translation that seems to sit differently.

You might begin to track the way in which you are looking at time. Perhaps this can look like asking yourself what the gifts of each of the Norns are on that particular day. You can look to see how they might arrive.

I like to call the Norns into my mind and then open myself up to any messages they might offer during the day. I then track these messages, act on them as appropriate, and then review the week to see how the Norns may have already shown themselves.

Reverence and Devotion

When I talk about working with godds, it is clear I am in devotion and not supplication. While I respect and honor deities, I do not offer things blindly or beyond what is available to me. Another way to say this is that I don't do things that I don't want to do

71

because it seems like it might be a holy act.

The Norns offer many things. They offer the lessons that life is complicated and made of many threads. Life is also short and measured, and you have no idea when the thread might be cut, so you need to act. With these things in mind, one of the best ways to be in devotion to the Norns is to live your life as best you can. Figure out what your values are, what your priorities are, and what you want to change about the way you live your life. For me, this has looked like a long and ongoing practice of introspection. This has looked like asking each Norn for their perspective on where I have been, what I am becoming, and what might be on its way. I can do this by:

- Journaling
- Divination – Runes, Tarot Cards, etc.
- Sitting in meditation with each Norn

One of the lessons of the Norns is that you have this wondrous fate and thread that connects to so many others. While we don't always know how we impact another human being, we can review our own thread, examine it, and decide if the way we are living is the best way. We can stop and consider how else we might show up well. In doing so, we are devoted not only to ourselves and healing our past but also to bringing in a better future, as well as creating a 'better' wyrd for future generations.

Of course, there are the things you can do that will help to ground your practice, things you likely already do for other deities or other energies:

- **Altar building** – Setting up an altar to the Norns is always nice and gives them a physical place in your home. It doesn't have to be complicated, nor does it have to be large. I have a clay carving and a piece of yarn from a ritual piece I did with them as my altar. You might also have a bowl of water for the Well of Urd. Or a symbol of the World Tree.

- **Offerings** – The offerings you might give to the Norns can vary based on your relationship and your work with them. Sometimes mine look like runes that I pull for the day or a question. Sometimes I add more yarn or string. And sometimes I offer a song or a breath.
- **Weaving** – It makes sense to figure out how to practice some weaving to really get into the energy of the Norns. Even if you're not destined to be a great weaver or artist, it can help to learn some basic movements of yarn or string as a meditative practice. And if that seems inaccessible, watching people weave via online tutorials works. And I can't weave to save me, so I braid things when I'm thinking of the Norns, with each strand being a connection to each Norn.

Devotion is the practice of showing up and showing up again. It is the practice of consistency and reciprocation in a relationship. There will be days when you are tired. There will be days when you are not inspired or excited. This is all part of the relationship-building and growing process.

While I do not propose that people move beyond what makes them comfortable, I would offer that making sacred is also a part of the word 'sacrifice.' This does not have to be painful but making a relationship holy sometimes does require you to give more than you usually do. And you should be in this giving practice because you want to give. When you begin to notice you are giving to get, then this is where things can get unbalanced, and you can get resentful.

Setting Expectations and Boundaries

To foster stronger connections with the godds and humans, it helps to start with a clear sense of boundaries and expectations.

Now, while it can be said that expectations of mystery are harder to pin down, you are in control of the expectations you can have for yourself. Let's look at this a little more closely. When establishing a relationship, you need to be clear about what you can and what you cannot or will not do.

- I can create an altar. It cannot be easy for others to see because I need privacy.
- I can sit at this altar daily, but only for five minutes.
- I will work with one Norn for a week at a time, then the fourth week is for all Norns.

I understand that this might seem a little prescriptive to some. You may want things to be more spontaneous and less (seemingly) rigid. That is entirely valid. If that's how you are feeling this week, I might offer that starting with a clear sense of your relationship will help you become more spontaneous.

It's common that working with deities can include the assumption that the godds will never let us down. As a result, we must work harder and give more. Though I have ascribed to this myself, it creates a power imbalance from the start. And that isn't how you want a relationship to start. At least, I don't think that's a good beginning.

Start with small things you know you can commit to. Be clear about what is comfortable and appropriate for your living situation. Not everyone is loud about their magickal practice. You don't have to be if you can't right now. Begin with a few things you can commit to and review them in a month or two to see how they're working. I find that the more I can be consistent with my practice, the richer it is. Sometimes the smallest promises yield the most significant gains. You will trust yourself in the relationship and the godds will know to trust you too.

When Things Are Quiet

No matter how consistent you are with your practice, there will be a point at which you might notice the godds aren't as interactive as they once were. This might come as a period of quiet, a lack of signs, or an overall feeling of stillness. You might feel uncomfortable, and it might feel like you missed something. After all, you are doing everything you said you would do. You are showing up and you are clear on what your expectations are for yourself. This happens sometimes. It might be a sign that you need to add more to your practice or that you need to take a break for a bit.

Check-in with yourself to see if you have been consistent with your practice. Sometimes when you're doing things for a while, it becomes second nature and easy to do without a lot of heart and emotion. It can help to return to the reasons why you're in this relationship to see if they still fit. Or do you need to adjust things? Do you want to try something else? Do you notice any patterns in the messages you get or the way things are showing up? Look back at your journal to see if there were signs along the way. Do another reading with some form of divination. Clean up your altar. Move the altar. Shift things to something different.

Sometimes, things just get in a rut and magickal practice is no different. You might find you just need to shift one small thing to get things moving again. Or you might just need to wait things out as not everything blooms all the time. It might just be a time when you need to rest and relax. Keep doing what you're doing, and things will return.

Do the Godds Get Mad?

It's not surprising that humans can quickly move on to thinking a godd is mad at them. And it's too bad that we've been in enough relationships with silent treatment that it's even a worry. I can't speak for the godds, but I can't imagine that beings with an infinite understanding of time and how our lives are likely to turn out would be mad for you missing a meditation day. Instead, I might ask myself if I have been upholding my promises to the godds. If I have, I will try my best to dismiss the human reaction of 'oh no, I did something wrong' and move back to being consistent.

If I have been out of integrity with my practice, then it's time to get things back on track. Again, I don't think godds get mad, but I do think they appreciate it when you do what you say you will do.

When It's Time to Move On...

Though there are deities you might work with your entire life, and the Norns seem to be ones that could be perfect for a lifetime, this isn't always the way things work. You might notice you are wary of your practice or that you're not getting what you want or need from the relationship. Again, you have human relationships to compare this to, so you are already well-equipped for this part. I would offer that if you feel ready to move on to another relationship or you feel like you need to step away for a bit, do that. It is just fine to step back from something that isn't working out.

You might interact with the Norns in some way to let them know you are stepping back. This might look like saying the words aloud and being straightforward if you are taking down altars or stopping certain practices. It doesn't have to be dramatic, though it might include a laying down of the thread that you were weaving with them. You can always put it away, as it will always be a part of you, even if it's not something you are holding onto right now.

I believe it's good magickal hygiene to be clear when stepping back from a relationship with deities. While there are deities that I work with regularly, there are some that I don't work with as much anymore. By offering a thank you and goodbye, I feel we're still on good terms. There are some breakups in which you can remain friends.

Practice: Sitting at the Base of the World Tree

A practice that might work for you to learn about the Norns works well if you have access to a tree. It doesn't have to be ash, nor does it have to be particularly big, but it needs to be something that you might assign the energy of Yggdrasil.

There are a few things I'd recommend with this tree. I would recommend starting to sit at the base of the tree regularly. You might sit there and journal about the Norns. You might sit there and journal about your life. Or you might choose to sit and call the Norns into your presence. You might ask them to come to visit with you as you seek to build a relationship with them. Remembering that relationships take time, and should, this might be an ongoing working over many months or years.

Another possibility is to find a plant that you might cultivate and nourish as a part of your practice with the Norns. This should be something that requires tending and water on a regular basis. This way, you can sit in the place of the Norns and tend to your own sort of world tree. Notice what happens as you take care of the roots and take care of a growing thing. How does this impact your daily life? How much of your life does it affect? What does it mean to you when you forget a day? What happens when you don't have anything to tend to and it gets dull?

Notice all of it. And consider what it would be like to sit by this tree/plant day and night while watching the movement of the world and its people. While it seems true that the Norns had travels and responsibilities that took them away from the tree, it is also said that this tree needed to be nourished no matter what – or else the tree's roots would rot.

Practice: Nourishing Your Roots

I also invite the possibility that nourishing your own roots is a wise practice when working with the Norns. The roots that have been there, are here, and that will (hopefully) continue to grow in the future require your attention. I encourage you to think about how your roots need to be tended. If you're not sure what this means, think about what you need to feel healthy and whole. What is your foundation? What are the things that support you? When you feel out of sorts, what have you neglected? If you're still unsure, let's work with a few things that are commonplace and you can extend from here when you get a clearer sense of your own needs. When I'm stuck, I tend to look at the categories of physical, mental, emotional, and spiritual.

- What could I do physically to support myself?
- What could I do mentally to support my mind?
- What could I do emotionally to support my emotional well-being?
- What could I do spiritually to support my practices and magick?

And when I am stumbling about how to care for myself, I look at myself like a child who can't put things into words as well as (I think) I can now.

- Have you slept?
- Have you eaten?
- Have you had water today?
- Have you showered?
- Have you taken your medications?
- Have you talked to someone you love?
- Have you been held?
- Have you shared your needs?
- Have you shared your feelings?

Caring for your roots can begin with going to bed earlier or eating one more vegetable a day. Or drinking a glass of water when you wake up. Start small and see how things feel. I notice that when I can be consistent about 'little' things, they become big things that support additional shifts in my life.

The act of caring for yourself is one that resounds in a practice with the Norns. After all, our actions impact our fate and the fates of others. While I do not believe *just* caring for ourselves is the answer to a better life or world, it is a part of caring for the collective. When you actively care for yourself, you will nourish the tree's roots that connect us all. You enable yourself to be a healthy part of the tree and when others do the same, it becomes a more effective, interdependent community.

Practice: Relationship Check-In

This might not seem like a practice you would see in a book about the godds. This sounds more like a couple's therapy practice, I know. To keep your relationship with the godds intact and healthy, I suggest regular check-ins to see how you feel and how things feel for the Norns too. This can be as simple as a weekly offering to them the questions: How are things going? How can I show up well?

Sit and listen to these answers. Act accordingly or decide what you can do to ensure things feel on track. And this might be a moment to be clear with your deities that you can't do a certain practice that week due to a busy schedule and that you'll get back on track. Or you need to change a certain practice because it's not working for you anymore. Check-ins go both ways. They are essential to making sure everyone is fulfilled.

Chapter 8

Meeting Your Personal Nornir & Allies

When looking at the various sources of information on the Norns, one thing keeps coming up about the Norns that isn't talked about as widely. Though it is agreed upon that the Norns are those who are determining fate and measuring the thread of a life, it is unclear if they show up at every single birth.

Some sources talk about how the Norns might show up at a birth, or they might send other beings or subordinates to the births. From my understanding, personal nornir might be assigned to each person during their lives. This seems to be in the translations by Snorri Sturluson, which I haven't referenced much in this book until this point, though those translations have influenced me. I tend to favor other translations of the *Poetic Edda*.

That said, this does bring up a point that if there are many norns (or nornir) available to people, then what about finding and meeting a personal norn who might offer you insight into your life choices?

Witnessing Your Births

According to Snorri Sturluson, an Icelandic historian and poet from the 13th century, there were norns that came to individual children at birth, and some of the norns were good and some were bad. If they were good, the child was good and would have a good life. If they were had, then the child was destined for bad things. [17] (Snorri also says that norns came from different races, while some were of elf or dwarf descent and others were divine.)

To me, it makes sense that a norn would come to a birth as they are the holders of that thread that encompasses a lifetime. It also makes sense that some children would fare well and badly from the time of birth. However, what is limiting about this detail is that it leaves out the idea of the child having agency in their lives.

Or does it? After all, one might only blame a norn for creating a 'bad' life if the life turned out in a way that wasn't expected. Is the 'bad' something that can be seen or recognized at birth? Or is it something that emerges? I don't have an answer here. But as you've already heard of norns being vengeful and difficult in stories, I wanted to offer it into the conversation.

The Dísir

The Norse magickal practice is vast and full of ideas that intersect with fate because it's everywhere and everything. The dís, for example, are spirits that are related to fate, with dísir being the plural form of the word. These spirits can be good or bad toward humans. They are often seen as female, with the possible translation of 'goddess.'

The dísir are also equated with or play the role of norns. They give an impression of great age, but by the time of the oldest surviving texts, their significance had become blurred and the word had lost almost all distinct meaning.[18]

In the modern era, where there is a lot of conversation about whether the gender binary is needed, I want to offer that this is where translations of texts become muddy for me. The translators are often prescribing their own ideas into the translations. From there, these ideas become common thoughts and are just accepted as a part of the mythology. This is not to say that I want to dismiss what is available in books, but that a reader might consider things might not be as narrow as they seem.

The dísir are also often described as a circle of female ancestors that protect humans. For some, this doesn't feel very comforting, so it might be more inclusive to expand this to those who birth or those who mother without being attached to gender.

One of my favorite practices in Norse magick is the creation of the dísir circle, wherein we call to the ancestors to stand around a circle for protection. In the context of fate, this might look like calling out to those who might want to protect us from any ill happenings that might harm us. That might harm our fate or impact our wyrd.

The way I picture it is that when these maternal beings stand around the outside of the circle, they are facing out and away to make sure the magick is held safe. For the magick of fate, it might be a good practice to call in these ancestors, no matter their gender presentation, to surround your work and your magick.

Travel to Meet Your Personal Nornir

If it resonates with you that there are many more norns than the three that get the most attention, you might find this practice helpful and expansive. This is a more modern practice that I have used to help me better understand myself and my place in this particular timeline.

Find a space in which you can rest and be uninterrupted. Bring with you a cloak or scarf and a journal. If you are someone who can get distracted easily, I suggest headphones or earplugs. This practice is powerful when things are as quiet as possible. (And if you are a being who needs some noise, I suggest Heilung, Wardruna, or Danheim as musical inspiration.)

Get into a comfortable space where you are either in quiet or listening to music. Put the cloak over your face and head so you are completely in darkness. Know that you are safe and surrounded by your ancestors and your allies.

In this place, I invite you to breathe into the space of your birth and your welcome into this world. Whether you know how it happened or not, travel back to when you were brought into this world, with the circumstances you know and all that you knew later.

Allow yourself to emerge into the bright light of being where your thread was woven into the wyrd. Open your inner eye or your inner knowing and see who was present at your birth. Look at the people who were living and breathing with you. Look at the ancestors who traveled to the place to welcome you into the world.

Feel into the experience and into who else might have been watching this momentous occasion. Perhaps the Norns? Perhaps another being who stands to the side of you? Drop into this place and feel into what energy is there and waiting for you. Who is watching over you? What might they offer in the thread that is yours?

If you can't feel or see a being, move to the thread that is being woven. What does it look like? What does it include? What does it feel like? What is the texture? Color? Weight? What does it include from previous histories? What is it missing?

Allow yourself to deepen into the possibility that you have another nornir that is part of this introduction to the world. That there is wisdom in your welcoming. That there is something so much bigger than you, asking you to be a part of this moment in time. In all times.

Once you have a sense of this being or energy or presence, you might want to stay for a moment to see what else arrives. And if it is still unclear, you can bring yourself back to your body and to your present moment. Remove the covering and open your eyes. Write down anything that seems important, even if it doesn't make sense. Return to this practice as you like.

But Was It Really Weaving?

Right as we get to the end of things, I want to name something that scholars have discussed: was weaving something that the Norns would have been doing? Translations talk about the fates of men not being woven, but rather carved into pieces of wood. These slips of wood were then put into the Well of Urd.

My guess is that the weaving and spinning of threads is a poetic approach to describing how fates are connected to each other. It makes sense to talk about weaving and then include female figures who are doing the weaving. The verb that is used in the *Poetic Edda* is one that means 'to twist', but that doesn't necessarily mean to spin or to weave.

Karen Bek-Pedersen's book *The Norns in Old Norse Mythology* and her writings online[19] consider this question very closely and do not offer any concrete conclusions. Another thought that Bek-Pedersen offers is that perhaps the Norns were not the creators of fate, but just the ones who fulfill it, thus if they are not weaving or spinning, they are still holding what needs to be held for humans and godds.

I want to offer that the poetry of weaving works for me and is very common in songs, stories, and other descriptions of the Norns. Just because it might not be true does not mean the imagery isn't real for some. As you have already noticed from my writing, it's the imagery that works for me. But I know I'm also considering how to move wooden tablets into my practice to expand my experience of the Norns.

Conclusion

Weaving Together

The way I see it is this (at least in this moment):

Urd is the energy of what we cannot change (the circumstances we were born into, the mistakes we and decisions we have already made, the moments we did or did not embrace).

Verdandi is the reminder that we only have moments (fleeting opportunities that we will miss, but will offer us chance after chance).

Skuld is the holder of what will arrive next (mysterious and unknowable, formed by decisions and the way other threads pull at us).

We have been woven and we will weave each moment as co-conspirators of our destiny. We walk together in this strange web of what is, what was, and what shall be. In these moments of realization, in these admissions of our part to play, we become the ones we have been waiting for. We are the ones we create and embrace, the ones we desire and the ones we dismiss.

Woven into these connections are the sticky and stringy parts: oppression of many forms, capitalism, climate change, pandemics, war, heartbreak, illness, misunderstandings, misgivings, missteps, and the best/worst of intentions. It's all of us. It's all of this world. It's the experience of being human, alive and attentive.

I invite the possibility that the Norns are watching over you and me. That they are doing what they have been doing for the stretches ahead and beyond this moment. The World Tree is watered, the threads are woven. The story continues.

What do we do with the time we have? With the measure we have been offered? With the talents and experiences that make us unique?

- What might you do now?
- What might you change?
- What can you look at more closely?
- What can you leave behind?

Take Your Place in the Web of Wyrd

Before you finish reading, I encourage you to sit with the Norns. It does not need to be fancy or proper. It can be a few minutes or an hour. But sit in the energy of these beings you have spent your time and attention to meet.

Close your eyes if that feels like the thing to do. Or keep your eyes open to the world around you, taking in every color and texture, sound and smell. Imagine the threads of your life stretching out from your body. These stretch out to your parents, your siblings, other family members, your partner(s), your friends, your teachers, your pets, your neighbors, your healthcare providers, and the people you have met in your life.

Take your time with this, this remembering of the threads that have been attached to you. All of the ways in which you have been impacted by others in small and large ways. And the way you have impacted the lives of others, in big and small ways. Notice the tension or the slack in the threads. The colors. The textures. The lengths of these threads. Notice them all. Notice how you are in the center of your life experience, but also play a role in the lives of others.

How does this feel to you? What do you notice? What is surprising? What feels like home? What requires attention? What asks for repair and reconciliation? Allow those answers to come and land as they do. With their clarity and their confusion, with their wisdom and their vagueness. Capture them in your heart or on paper.

In the days to come, look around for the threads that connect you to others. Look for threads and weaving to show up in your life. Recognize when the Norns show up in small ways, reminding you that you are a part of this weave of life for a reason and likely for many reasons.

A Reminder from a Runic Stick

One of the best things I came upon in my research is something I want to leave with you in the end (or the beginning) of your relationship with the Norns. According to Bek-Pedersen, Søndre Engelgården found a runic stick in about c. 1225 to 1250[20], bearing an inscription that contained the nornir. While there is more context in Bek-Pedersen's book, I leave this for your nourishment and as an expansion of how the Norns might arrive for you. (As they have for me.)

The ancient wind of the cliff-nornir [my thoughts] turned very early for me towards the beautiful, harmful fir-tree [woman] carrying fire [gold] from the deep fish-ground [sea]. They [the thoughts] have been held fast by magic. Love conquers everything, let us surrender to love, held fast by magic. Love conquers everything, let us surrender to love.[21]

This love charm contains multitudes of meaning and poetry, just as was typical in the writing. But it arrives as a reminder of the heaviness of thoughts and how they can be held by magick, and we are invited to surrender to love.

I know this is not a direct quote of the Norns, nor is it even connecting the Norns to love magick, but it does link back to fate and the way it also asks us to surrender by meeting it, however it has been woven for us.

To the Norns, to the Wyrd Sisters, the ones who reside at the base of the World Tree, I offer you my gratitude and my consolation. What a role it is to weave, measure, and cut the threads of life. I honor this life in the ways that feel right and holy. I honor this lifetime as a gift.

To those in the hall beneath the tree, I offer you acceptance, attention, and trust.

I offer you my mind, my heart, and my actions.

Hail the three sisters. Hail the Norns.

Endnotes

1. Author's note: I use 'godds' as a more gender-full and inclusive word for deities
2. Lindow, J., *Norse Mythology*, p.243
3. Lindow, J., *Norse Mythology*, p.243
4. Bek-Pedersen., *The Norns in Old Norse Mythology*, p.1
5. Crossley-Holland, K., *The Norse Myths*, p.15
6. Bek-Pedersen., *The Norns in Old Norse Mythology*, p.15
7. Taunton, G., *Fate and the Twilight of the Gods*, p.18
8. Orchard, A., *Dictionary of Northern Mythology*, p.79
9. Bosworth, J. and Northcote Toller, T., *An Anglo-Saxon Dictionary; https://bosworthtoller.com/36952*
10. https://www.americanscientist.org/article/understanding-the-butterfly-effect
11. Smith, R., *The Way of Fire and Ice*. p.32
12. https://karitauring.com/oorlog-and-wyrd/
13. http://www.reclaimingquarterly.org/86/rq-86-aspect-intro.html
14. https://www.goodreads.com/quotes/7526239-when-a-person-has-a-reaction-to-something-in-their
15. Orchard, A., *Dictionary of Norse Myth and Legend*, p.151
16. https://www.ncbi.nlm.nih.gov/pmc/articles/PMC3652533/
17. Heath, Cat., *Elves, Witches & Gods: Spinning Old Heathen Magic in the Modern Day*. p.100
18. de Vries, J., *Altgermanische Religionsgeschichte*, 2 vols., vol. 2, 2nd ed. Berlin: de Gruyter, 1957, repr. as 3rd ed. 1970, p.298
19. http://web.archive.org/web/20080926172355/http:/www.dur.ac.uk/medieval.www/sagaconf/bek.htm
20. Bek-Pedersen, K., *The Norns in Old Norse Mythology*, p.21
21. Bek-Pedersen, K., *The Norns in Old Norse Mythology*, p.21

Resources & Bibliography

Resources

Bek-Pedersen, Karen. *The Norns in Old Norse Mythology*
Daimler, Morgan. *Pantheon - The Norse*
Larrington, Carolyn. *The Poetic Edda*
McCoy, Daniel. *The Viking Spirit*
Smith, Ryan. *The Way of Fire and Ice*
Taunton, Gwendolyn. *Fate and the Twilight of the Gods*

Bibliography

Andrsson, Wíghearðr T. *Völuspá and Hávamál: Nordic Wisdom in English, Old Norse, and Younger Futhark*
Bek-Pedersen, Karen. *The Norns in Old Norse Mythology*
Bellow, Henry A. *The Poetic Edda*
Crawford, Jackson. *The Poetic Edda: Stories of the Norse Gods and Heroes*
Crossley-Holland, Kevin. *The Norse Myths*
Heath, Cat. *Elves, Witches & Gods: Spinning Old Heathen Magic in the Modern Day*
Hollander, Lee M. *The Poetic Edda*
Larrington, Carolyn. *The Poetic Edda*
Lindow, John. *Norse Mythology: A Guide to the Gods, Heroes, Rituals, and Beliefs*
Orchard, Andy. *Dictionary of Norse Myth and Legend*
Sigfusson, Saemund, Sturluson, Snorri, Thorpe, Benjamin, Blackwell, I.A. *The Poetic Edda & The Prose Edda (Complete Edition): The Elder Saemundar Edda: Baldr's Dreams, Loki's Altercation + The Younger Snorri's Edda: Of Odin, Of Thor, Of Ragnarok, Gylfi's Journey To Asgard*
Simek, Rudolf. *Dictionary of Northern Mythology*
Smith, Ryan. *The Way of Fire and Ice*
Taunton, Gwendolyn. *Fate and the Twilight of the Gods*

About the Author

Irisanya Moon is a priestess, teacher, and initiate in the Reclaiming tradition. She has taught classes and camps around the world, including in the US, Canada, UK, and Australia. Irisanya writes a regular blog, *Charged by the Goddess*, for Patheos.

You can find out more about Irisanya's writing and teaching at: www.irisanyamoon.com

You can find her blog at: https://www.patheos.com/blogs/chargedbythegoddess

Books by Irisanya Moon:

Earth Spirit
Gaia: Saving Her, Saving Ourselves
Honoring the Wild: Reclaiming Witchcraft & Environmental Activism

Pagan Portals
Reclaiming Witchcraft
Aphrodite - Encountering the Goddess of Love & Beauty & Initiation
Iris - Goddess of the Rainbow and Messenger of the Godds
The Norns - Weavers of Fate and Magick

Practically Pagan
An Alternative Guide to Health & Well-being

You may also like...

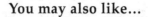

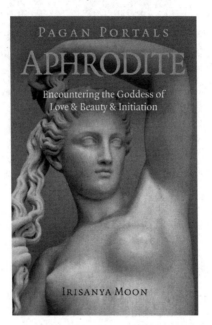

Aphrodite - Encountering the Goddess of
Love & Beauty & Initiation

*Aphrodite is an often misunderstood goddess, one who is easy
to relegate to the love goddess role, but who also shows up as an
initiator and (some might say) troublemaker. In this book, we seek to
travel the complexity of a goddess who was born on sea foam and who
inspires beauty and love, all the while offering a hand toward each
one of us to celebrate our full* hearts.

978-1-78904-347-1 (Paperback)
978-1-78904-348-8 (e-book)

About the Author

MOON BOOKS
PAGANISM & SHAMANISM

What is Paganism? A religion, a spirituality, an alternative belief system, nature worship? You can find support for all these definitions (and many more) in dictionaries, encyclopaedias, and text books of religion, but subscribe to any one and the truth will evade you. Above all Paganism is a creative pursuit, an encounter with reality, an exploration of meaning and an expression of the soul. Druids, Heathens, Wiccans and others, all contribute their insights and literary riches to the Pagan tradition. Moon Books invites you to begin or to deepen your own encounter, right here, right now.

If you have enjoyed this book, why not tell other readers by posting a review on your preferred book site.

Recent bestsellers from Moon Books are:

Journey to the Dark Goddess
How to Return to Your Soul
Jane Meredith
Discover the powerful secrets of the Dark Goddess and
transform your depression, grief and pain into healing
and integration.
Paperback: 978-1-84694-677-6 ebook: 978-1-78099-223-5

Shamanic Reiki
Expanded Ways of Working with Universal Life Force Energy
Llyn Roberts, Robert Levy
Shamanism and Reiki are each powerful ways of healing; together,
their power multiplies. *Shamanic Reiki* introduces techniques to
help healers and Reiki practitioners tap ancient healing wisdom.
Paperback: 978-1-84694-037-8 ebook: 978-1-84694-650-9

Pagan Portals – The Awen Alone
Walking the Path of the Solitary Druid
Joanna van der Hoeven
An introductory guide for the solitary Druid, *The Awen Alone* will
accompany you as you explore, and seek out your own place
within the natural world.
Paperback: 978-1-78279-547-6 ebook: 978-1-78279-546-9

A Kitchen Witch's World of Magical Herbs & Plants
Rachel Patterson
A journey into the magical world of herbs and plants, filled with
magical uses, folklore, history and practical magic. By popular
writer, blogger and kitchen witch, Tansy Firedragon.
Paperback: 978-1-78279-621-3 ebook: 978-1-78279-620-6

Medicine for the Soul
The Complete Book of Shamanic Healing
Ross Heaven
All you will ever need to know about shamanic healing and how to
become your own shaman...
Paperback: 978-1-78099-419-2 ebook: 978-1-78099-420-8

Shaman Pathways – The Druid Shaman
Exploring the Celtic Otherworld
Danu Forest
A practical guide to Celtic shamanism with exercises and
techniques as well as traditional lore for exploring the Celtic
Otherworld.
Paperback: 978-1-78099-615-8 ebook: 978-1-78099-616-5

Traditional Witchcraft for the Woods and Forests
A Witch's Guide to the Woodland with Guided Meditations and
Pathworking
Mélusine Draco
A Witch's guide to walking alone in the woods, with guided
meditations and pathworking.
Paperback: 978-1-84694-803-9 ebook: 978-1-84694-804-6

Wild Earth, Wild Soul
A Manual for an Ecstatic Culture
Bill Pfeiffer
Imagine a nature-based culture so alive and so connected,
spreading like wildfire. This book is the first flame...
Paperback: 978-1-78099-187-0 ebook: 978-1-78099-188-7

Naming the Goddess
Trevor Greenfield
Naming the Goddess is written by over eighty adherents and
scholars of Goddess and Goddess Spirituality.
Paperback: 978-1-78279-476-9 ebook: 978-1-78279-475-2

Shapeshifting into Higher Consciousness
Heal and Transform Yourself and Our World with Ancient
Shamanic and Modern Methods
Llyn Roberts
Ancient and modern methods that you can use every day to
transform yourself and make a positive difference in the world.
Paperback: 978-1-84694-843-5 ebook: 978-1-84694-844-2

Readers of ebooks can buy or view any of these bestsellers by
clicking on the live link in the title. Most titles are published in
paperback and as an ebook. Paperbacks are available in traditional
bookshops. Both print and ebook formats are available online.

Find more titles and sign up to our readers' newsletter at
http://www.johnhuntpublishing.com/paganism
Follow us on Facebook at https://www.facebook.com/MoonBooks
and Twitter at https://twitter.com/MoonBooksJHP

About the Author